COUNTRY
COOKING

EDITORIAL
U.S. Editor: Carol Spier
Food Editor: Rachel Blackmore
Assistant Food Editor: Anneka Mitchell
Home Economist: Donna Hay
Recipe Development: Sheryle Eastwood,
Carolyn Fienberg, Doreen Badger (Bread
Research Institute of Australia Inc)
Editorial Coordinator: Margaret Kelly
Subeditor: Ella Martin

PHOTOGRAPHY
Ashley Mackevicius

STYLING
Carolyn Fienberg, Anna Philips, Wendy
Berecry (cover)

PRODUCTION
Tara Barrett
Chris Hatcher

COVER DESIGN
Frank Pithers

DESIGN AND PRODUCTION
MANAGER
Nadia Sbisa

PUBLISHER
Philippa Sandall

COUNTRY COOKING
Includes Index
ISBN 1 56197 037 9

Published by J.B. Fairfax Press Inc.
15 West 26th Street
New York, New York 10010

Formatted by J.B. Fairfax Press Pty Ltd
Printed by Toppan Printing Co, Hong Kong

USEFUL INFORMATION

Microwave: Where microwave instructions occur in this book a microwave oven with a 650 watt output has been used. Wattage on domestic microwave ovens varies between 500 and 700 watts, and it may be necessary to vary the cooking times slightly depending on your oven.

Canned foods: Can sizes vary between countries and manufacturers. You may find the quantities in this book are slightly different from what is available. Purchase and use the can size nearest to the suggested size in the recipe.

COUNTRY

freshly
BAKED

Cakes and cookies

home
COOKING

Roasts, casseroles and stews

harvest
FESTIVAL

*Vegetables, grains,
eggs and cheese*

the pantry
SHELF

Jams, pickles and chutneys

COOKING

country KITCHEN

Loaves, rolls and scones

a day in the COUNTRY

The picnic hamper

the pastry CRUST

Pies and tarts

full of GOODNESS

Soups for all seasons

family FAVORITES

Desserts

INDEX

RESOURCES
ACKNOWLEDGMENTS

freshly BAKED

Cakes and cookies

*B*ring back memories of days gone by with the aroma of freshly baked cakes and cookies. When you see how easy the following recipes are, you will reach for the cake pans and cookie sheets. Chocolate Chip or Anzac Cookies, or Dundee Cake – no matter what you choose, your family and friends will be delighted!

*Top: Wheat weaving 'House Blessing'
Right: Apricot Banana Loaf, Chocolate Chip
Cookies, Eccles Cookies, Victoria Layer
Cake (all recipes pages 6 and 7)*

VICTORIA LAYER CAKE

Named after Queen Victoria, the Victoria Layer Cake was served at her afternoon tea parties. The cake, usually filled with raspberry jam, soon became popular throughout the country. Our version includes cream, but for something simpler, you might prefer it in its original form – filled with jam and lightly dusted with confectioners' sugar.

Makes an 8 in/20 cm round cake
Oven temperature 350°F/180°C

- [ ] **4 eggs**
- [ ] **³/4 cup/170 g superfine sugar**
- [ ] **1 cup/125 g self-rising flour**
- [ ] **4 teaspoons corn starch**
- [ ] **¹/3 cup warm water**
- [ ] **1¹/2 teaspoons melted butter**
- [ ] **4 teaspoons confectioners' sugar, sifted**

FILLING
- [ ] **¹/2 cup/155 g strawberry jam**
- [ ] **¹/2 cup/125 mL heavy cream, whipped**
- [ ] **4 teaspoons confectioners' sugar, sifted**

1   Place eggs in a large mixing bowl and beat until thick and creamy. Gradually add sugar, beating well after each addition. Continue beating until mixture becomes thick. This will take about 10 minutes.
2   Sift together flour and corn starch over egg mixture and fold in. Stir in water and melted butter.
3   Divide batter evenly between two greased and lined 8 in/20 cm round pans. Bake for 20-25 minutes or until cake shrinks slightly from sides of cake pan and springs back when touched with the fingertips. Leave in cake pans for 5 minutes before turning onto a wire rack to cool.
4   To assemble, spread one layer with jam, then top with whipped cream and remaining layer. Sprinkle top of cake with confectioners' sugar and serve.
Passion Fruit Layer Cake: Spread one layer with lemon curd, then top with whipped cream and remaining layer. Spread top of cake with passion fruit icing: To make passion fruit icing, combine 1 tablespoon softened butter and ¹/4 cup passion fruit pulp with 1 cup confectioners' sugar, sifted, and mix with enough water to make an icing of spreadable consistency.

CHOCOLATE CHIP COOKIES

Makes 40
Oven temperature 400°F/200°C

- [ ] **1 cup/250 g butter, softened**
- [ ] **2 teaspoons vanilla extract**
- [ ] **2 cups/350 g brown sugar**
- [ ] **2 eggs**
- [ ] **2 cups/250 g flour, sifted**
- [ ] **1 cup/125 g self-rising flour, sifted**
- [ ] **2 cups/185 g shredded coconut**
- [ ] **8 oz/250 g choc chips**

1   Place butter, vanilla extract and sugar in a mixing bowl and beat until light and fluffy. Add eggs one at a time, beating well after each addition.
2   Stir in flours, coconut and choc chips. Roll heaped spoonfuls of mixture into balls, place on well-greased cookie sheets and flatten slightly with a spatula. Bake for 12-15 minutes. Remove from oven and leave on cookie sheets for a few minutes before removing to wire racks to cool completely.

ECCLES COOKIES

Makes 16
Oven temperature 400°F/200°C

- [ ] **24 oz/750 g prepared or ready-rolled shortcrust pastry**
- [ ] **4 teaspoons superfine sugar**
- [ ] **pinch ground nutmeg**
- [ ] **pinch ground allspice**

FRUIT FILLING
- [ ] **¹/4 cup superfine sugar**
- [ ] **2 tablespoons/30 g butter**
- [ ] **4 oz/125 g currants**
- [ ] **1 oz/30 g candied fruit, chopped**
- [ ] **¹/2 teaspoon ground allspice**
- [ ] **¹/2 teaspoon ground nutmeg**

1   To make filling, place sugar and butter in a saucepan and cook over a low heat until butter melts. Stir in currants, candied fruit, allspice and nutmeg and cook for 2-3 minutes longer. Remove from heat and set aside to cool.
2   Roll out pastry to a ¹/8 in/3 mm thickness. Using a 4 in/10 cm cookie cutter, cut out rounds. Place a teaspoon of fruit mixture in center of each pastry round. Fold pastry over filling and pinch edges together. Turn rounds over so edges are facing

downwards and flatten each gently using a rolling pin.
3   Make a small hole in the top of each cookie. Combine sugar, nutmeg and allspice and sprinkle over cookies. Place on a greased cookie sheet and bake for 12-15 minutes, or until pastry is golden and cooked.

RICH CHOCOLATE CAKE

Makes an 8 in/ 20 cm round cake
Oven temperature 350°F/180°C

- [ ] **12 tablespoons/185 g butter, softened**
- [ ] **1 teaspoon vanilla extract**
- [ ] **1¹/4 cups/280 g superfine sugar**
- [ ] **3 eggs**
- [ ] **3 oz/90 g semisweet chocolate, melted and cooled**
- [ ] **1³/4 cups/220 g flour**
- [ ] **2 teaspoons baking powder**
- [ ] **¹/4 cup/30 g cocoa powder**
- [ ] **³/4 cup/185 mL milk**
- [ ] **¹/4 cup strawberry jam**

CHOCOLATE BUTTER ICING
- [ ] **¹/2 cup/125 g butter, softened**
- [ ] **3¹/2 oz/100 g semisweet chocolate, melted and cooled**
- [ ] **2 egg yolks**
- [ ] **¹/2 cup/75 g confectioners' sugar, sifted**

1   Place butter and vanilla extract in a large mixing bowl and beat until light and fluffy. Gradually add sugar, beating well after each addition until mixture is creamy.
2   Beat in eggs one at a time, then mix in chocolate. Sift together flour, baking powder and cocoa powder. Fold flour mixture and milk alternately into chocolate mixture.
3   Spoon cake batter into a greased and lined deep 8 in/20 cm round cake pan and bake for 50-55 minutes, or until cooked when tested with a skewer. Leave for 5 minutes before turning onto a wire rack to cool completely.
4   To make icing, place butter in a mixing bowl and beat until light and fluffy. Add chocolate, egg yolks and confectioners' sugar and beat until smooth.
5   Split cold cake in half horizontally and layer together with jam. Spread icing over top and sides of cake.

Rich Chocolate Cake

APRICOT BANANA LOAF

*A wholesome loaf that improves
if kept for a day or two before
cutting. Serve in slices, lightly
spread with butter.*

Makes 1 loaf
Oven temperature 350°F/180°C

- ☐ ¹/₂ cup/125 g butter, softened
- ☐ 1 cup/250 g sugar
- ☐ 1 egg
- ☐ 3 ripe bananas, mashed
- ☐ 1 cup/125 g self-rising flour
- ☐ 1 cup/155 g whole wheat flour
- ☐ 1 teaspoon baking powder
- ☐ 1 teaspoon baking soda
- ☐ 1 teaspoon ground cardamom
- ☐ ¹/₂ teaspoon ground nutmeg
- ☐ ¹/₂ teaspoon ground allspice
- ☐ ¹/₂ cup/125 mL milk
- ☐ 5 oz/155 g dried apricots,
  chopped
- ☐ 3 oz/90 g pecans, chopped

1   Place butter in a bowl and beat until
light and fluffy. Gradually add sugar, beating
well after each addition until mixture is
creamy.
2   Beat in egg, then mix in bananas. Sift
together self-rising and whole wheat
flours, baking soda, baking powder,
cardamom, nutmeg and allspice into a
bowl. Return any chaff to flour mixture.
Fold flour mixture and milk alternately into
banana mixture, then mix in apricots and
pecans.
3   Spoon batter into a greased and lined
5 x 9 in/14 x 21 cm loaf pan and bake for
1¹/₄ hours or until cooked when tested with
a skewer. Stand in pan for 5 minutes
before turning onto a wire rack to cool
completely.

'Miss Dorothy'

DUNDEE CAKE

This traditional Scottish recipe, dating right back to the eighteenth century, is characterized by the almonds that decorate the top of the cake.

Makes an 8 in/20 cm round cake
Oven temperature 300°F/150°C

- ☐ **1 cup/250 g butter, softened**
- ☐ **1 teaspoon rum extract**
- ☐ **1 cup/220 g superfine sugar**
- ☐ **4 eggs, lightly beaten**
- ☐ **2 cups/250 g flour**
- ☐ **1 teaspoon baking powder**
- ☐ **$^1/_4$ cup/30 g corn starch**
- ☐ **8 oz/250 g raisins**
- ☐ **8 oz/250 g currants**
- ☐ **4 oz/125 g candied fruit**
- ☐ **4 oz/125 g slivered almonds**
- ☐ **2 oz/60 g glace cherries, halved**
- ☐ **2 teaspoons finely grated orange rind**
- ☐ **4 teaspoons freshly squeezed orange juice**
- ☐ **$1^1/_2$ oz/45 g blanched almonds**

1 Place butter and rum extract into a large mixing bowl and beat until light and fluffy. Gradually add sugar, beating well after each addition until mixture is creamy.
2 Add eggs one at a time, beating well after each addition. Sift together flour, baking powder and corn starch, then fold into butter mixture.
3 Stir in raisins, currants, candied fruit, slivered almonds, cherries, orange rind and orange juice. Spoon mixture into a greased and lined deep 8in/20 cm round cake pan. Decorate top of cake with blanched almonds, arranged in rings, and bake for 2$^1/_2$-3 hours, or until done when tested with a skewer. Set aside to cool in pan before turning out.

Spoon mixture into a greased and lined deep 8 in/20 cm round cake pan.

Decorate the top of the cake with almonds, arranged in rings.

Canisters and table Country Furniture Antiques *Picture and flowers Linen & Lace*

AFGHAN COOKIES

Makes 30
Oven temperature 400°F/200°C

- ☐ **13 tablespoons/200 g butter, softened**
- ☐ **1 teaspoon vanilla extract**
- ☐ **¹/₂ cup/100 g superfine sugar**
- ☐ **1¹/₂ cups/185 g flour**
- ☐ **1 teaspoon baking powder**
- ☐ **4 teaspoons cocoa powder**
- ☐ **1¹/₂ cups/90 g cornflakes, crushed**
- ☐ **3 tablespoons raisins, chopped**
- ☐ **slivered almonds**

CHOCOLATE ICING
- ☐ **1 tablespoon/15 g butter, softened**
- ☐ **4 teaspoons cocoa powder**
- ☐ **1 cup/155 g confectioners' sugar, sifted**
- ☐ **3-4 teaspoons water**

1 Place butter and vanilla extract in a mixing bowl and beat until light and fluffy. Gradually add sugar, beating well after each addition until mixture is creamy.

2 Sift together flour, baking powder and cocoa powder. Stir into butter mixture, then fold in cornflakes and rasins. Place heaped spoonfuls of mixture onto greased cookie sheets and bake for 12-15 minutes. Remove cookies and cool on wire racks.

3 To make icing, combine butter and cocoa powder with confectioners' sugar in a small bowl and mix in enough water to make an icing of spreadable consistency.

4 Place a teaspoon of icing on each cookie and sprinkle with almonds. Set aside until icing hardens. Store in an airtight container.

MELTING MOMENTS

Makes 24
Oven temperature 350°F/180°C

- ☐ **1 cup/250 g butter, softened**
- ☐ **¹/₃ cup/50 g confectioners' sugar, sifted**
- ☐ **1 cup/125 g corn starch**
- ☐ **1 cup/125 g flour**

LEMON CREAM
- ☐ **4 tablespoons/60 g butter, softened**
- ☐ **¹/₂ cup/75 g confectioners' sugar**
- ☐ **2 teaspoons finely grated lemon rind**
- ☐ **4 teaspoons lemon juice**

1 Place butter and confectioners' sugar in a large mixing bowl and beat until light and fluffy. Sift together corn starch and flour and stir into butter mixture.

2 Spoon mixture into a large piping bag fitted with a large star nozzle and pipe small rosettes on greased cookie sheets, leaving space between each rosette. Bake for 15-20 minutes or until pale golden. Cool on cookie sheets.

3 To make Lemon Cream, place butter in a mixing bowl and beat until light and fluffy. Gradually add sugar and beat until creamy. Stir in lemon rind and lemon juice. Using Lemon Cream, join flat sides of cookies. Store in an airtight container.

ORANGE POPPY SEED CAKE

Makes an 8 in/20 cm ring cake
Oven temperature 350°F/180°C

- [ ] ⅓ **cup poppy seeds**
- [ ] ¼ **cup freshly squeezed orange juice**
- [ ] **125 g plain yogurt**
- [ ] **12 tablespoons/185 g butter, softened**
- [ ] **4 teaspoons finely grated orange rind**
- [ ] **1 cup/220 g superfine sugar**
- [ ] **3 eggs**
- [ ] **2 cups/250 g self-rising flour, sifted**

1 Combine poppy seeds, orange juice and yogurt in a bowl and set aside to stand for 1 hour.
2 Place butter and orange rind in a large mixing bowl and beat until light and fluffy. Gradually add sugar, beating well after each addition until mixture is creamy.
3 Add eggs one at a time, beating well after each addition. Fold flour and poppy seed mixture alternately into butter mixture.
4 Spoon batter into a greased 8 in/20 cm bundt pan. Bake for 35-40 minutes, or until done when tested with a skewer. Leave in cake pan 5 minutes before turning onto a wire rack to cool.

MADEIRA CAKE

Makes a 9 in/23 cm square cake
Oven temperature 325°F/160°C

- [ ] **1 cup/250 g butter, softened**
- [ ] **2 teaspoons vanilla extract**
- [ ] **1 teaspoon finely grated lemon rind**
- [ ] **2 cups/440 g superfine sugar**
- [ ] **6 eggs**
- [ ] **1½ cups/185 g flour**
- [ ] **1 cup/125 g self-rising flour**
- [ ] **250 g plain yogurt**

LEMON ICING
- [ ] **1½ cups/220 g confectioners' sugar, sifted**
- [ ] **4 teaspoons lemon juice**
- [ ] **2 tablespoons/30 g butter, softened**
- [ ] **3 tablespoons shredded coconut, toasted**

1 Place butter, vanilla extract and lemon rind in a large mixing bowl and beat until light and fluffy. Gradually add sugar, beating well after each addition until mixture is creamy.
2 Add eggs one at a time, beating well after each addition. Sift flours together. Fold flour mixture and yogurt alternately into butter mixture. Spoon batter into a greased and lined deep 9 in/23 cm square cake pan. Bake for 1 hour or until cake is done when tested with a skewer. Leave in pan for 10 minutes before turning onto a wire rack to cool.
3 To make icing, place confectioners' sugar, lemon juice and butter in a bowl and mix until smooth. Add a little more lemon juice if necessary. Spread icing over cold cake and sprinkle with coconut.

Right: Afghan Cookies, Melting Moments, Ginger Snaps (page 12)
Below: Orange Poppy Seed Cake, Madeira Cake

GINGER SNAPS

As these cookies cool they become very crisp.

Makes 45
Oven temperature 350°F/180°C

- ☐ **1 cup/170 g brown sugar**
- ☐ **1 tablespoon ground ginger**
- ☐ **2 cups/250 g flour, sifted**
- ☐ **¹/₂ cup/125 g butter**
- ☐ **1 cup/360 g light molasses**
- ☐ **1 teaspoon baking soda**

1 Combine brown sugar, ginger and flour in a mixing bowl.
2 Place butter and molasses in a saucepan and cook over a low heat until butter melts. Stir in baking soda. Pour into dry ingredients and mix until smooth.
3 Drop teaspoons of mixture onto greased cookie sheets. Bake for 10-12 minutes or until golden. Remove from oven, loosen with a spatula and cool on cookie sheets. Store in an airtight container.

ANZAC COOKIES

Named after the Australian and New Zealand Army Corps (ANZAC) which fought at Gallipoli, these delicious crunchy cookies were baked at home and remained fresh on the long sea journey to the troops.

Makes 30
Oven temperature 325°F/160°C

- ☐ **1 cup/90 g quick-cooking rolled oats**
- ☐ **1 cup/90 g shredded coconut**
- ☐ **1 cup/125 g flour, sifted**
- ☐ **³/₄ cup/170 g superfine sugar**
- ☐ **¹/₂ cup/125 g butter**
- ☐ **1 tablespoon light molasses**
- ☐ **¹/₄ cup water**
- ☐ **¹/₂ teaspoon baking soda**

1 Place oats, coconut, flour and sugar in a mixing bowl and mix to combine.

2 Melt butter in a saucepan. Remove pan from heat and stir in molasses, water and baking soda. Pour into dry ingredients and mix well to combine.
3 Place heaped teaspoons of mixture on well-greased cookie sheets. Bake for 15-20 minutes. Remove from oven and leave on cookie sheets for 3 minutes before removing to wire racks to cool. Store in an airtight container.

APPLE SPICE CAKE

Makes an 8 in/20 cm round cake
Oven temperature 350°F/180°C

- ☐ **¹/₂ cup/125 g butter, softened**
- ☐ **1 teaspoon vanilla extract**
- ☐ **²/₃ cup/145 g superfine sugar**
- ☐ **2 eggs**
- ☐ **2 cups/250 g flour**
- ☐ **1 tablespoon baking powder**
- ☐ **¹/₂ cup/125 mL milk**

APPLE TOPPING
- ☐ **2 tablespoons/30 g butter**
- ☐ **1 green apple, cored, peeled and thinly sliced**
- ☐ **4 teaspoons superfine sugar**
- ☐ **2 teaspoons cinnamon**

1 To make topping, melt butter in a skillet and cook apples over a medium heat for 3-5 minutes or until tender-crisp. Remove pan from heat and set aside.
2 Place butter and vanilla extract in a mixing bowl and beat until light and fluffy. Gradually add sugar, beating well after each addition until mixture is creamy.
3 Add eggs one at a time, beating well after each addition. Sift together flour and baking powder. Fold flour mixture and milk alternately into creamed mixture. Spoon batter into a greased and lined deep 8 in/20 cm round cake pan.
4 Arrange apple mixture on top of cake. Combine sugar and cinnamon and sprinkle over top of cake. Bake for 40-45 minutes, or until done when tested with a skewer. Leave in pan for 5 minutes before turning onto a wire rack to cool.

Biscuit jar Country Furniture Antiques Butter container Country Store Antiques

HONEY CAKE

Honey Cake was a popular delicacy with the Ancient Greeks who believed that honey contained life-promoting properties. The Romans also served Honey Cake and it has remained popular throughout the centuries. If you use a flavored honey, such as clover, your cake will have a distinctive taste.

Makes an 8 in/20 cm square cake
Oven temperature 350°F/180°C

- [ ] $^1/_2$ cup/125 g butter, softened
- [ ] $^3/_4$ cup/125 g brown sugar
- [ ] 2 eggs
- [ ] 3 tablespoons honey
- [ ] 1 cup/125 g flour
- [ ] 1 cup/125 g self-rising flour
- [ ] 1 teaspoon baking powder
- [ ] $^1/_2$ cup/125 mL milk

HONEY FROSTING
- [ ] 3 tablespoons/45 g butter
- [ ] 4 oz/125 g cream cheese, softened
- [ ] 3 tablespoons honey, warmed
- [ ] nutmeg

1   Place butter in a large mixing bowl and beat until light and fluffy. Gradually add sugar, beating well after each addition until mixture is creamy.

2   Add eggs one at a time, beating well after each addition, then stir in honey. Sift together flours and baking powder. Fold flour mixture and milk alternately into butter mixture.

3   Spoon batter into a greased and lined 8 in/20 cm square cake pan. Bake for 35-40 minutes or until cake is done when tested with a skewer. Leave in cake pan for 5 minutes before turning onto a wire rack to cool.

4   To make frosting, place butter and cream cheese in a mixing bowl and beat until light and fluffy. Beat in honey and spread frosting over top of cooled cake. Sprinkle with nutmeg.

Apple Spice Cake, Honey Cake, Anzac Cookies

home
COOKING

Roasts, casseroles and stews

*T*empt their tastebuds with these
mouthwatering meals, cooked slowly in
the oven or simmered gently on top of
the stove. This chapter is full of country
goodness with delicious meals such as
Farmhouse Chicken Casserole,
Lamb Pot Roast and Roast Turkey.

Top: Wheat weaving 'Mordiford'
Left: Crusty Steak and Kidney Pie (page 16),
Farmhouse Chicken Casserole (page 17),
Lamb Pot Roast (page 16)

CRUSTY STEAK AND KIDNEY PIE

This modern version of steak and kidney pudding is just as tasty as the original, but easier to make and lighter to eat.

Serves 4
Oven temperature 350°F/180°C

- ☐ **1 lb/500 g flank steak**
- ☐ **3 lamb kidneys**
- ☐ **¹/₄ cup/60 g butter**
- ☐ **1 onion, chopped**
- ☐ **3 slices bacon, chopped**
- ☐ **2-3 tablespoons flour**
- ☐ **³/₄ cup/185 mL beef stock**
- ☐ **¹/₄ cup/60 mL red wine**
- ☐ **4 teaspoons tomato paste**
- ☐ **¹/₂ teaspoon sugar**
- ☐ **4 teaspoons finely chopped fresh parsley**
- ☐ **freshly ground black pepper**

SOUR CREAM CRUST
- ☐ **¹/₂ cup/125 g butter, softened**
- ☐ **1¹/₄ cups/300 g sour cream**
- ☐ **1 egg**
- ☐ **1¹/₂ cups/185 g self-rising flour**
- ☐ **4 teaspoons finely chopped fresh thyme**

1　Trim meat of all visible fat and cut into 1 in/2.5 cm pieces. Trim kidneys of all visible fat and soak in salted water for 10 minutes. Wipe dry with paper towels. Slash skin on rounded side of each kidney and draw it back on each side until it is attached by the core only. Draw out as much core as possible and cut, with skin, close to kidney. Cut each kidney into slices.
2　Melt 2 tablespoons/30 g butter in a large saucepan and cook meat in batches until browned on all sides. Remove from pan and set aside. Add kidney to pan and cook for 1-2 minutes to seal. Remove from pan and set aside. Stir in onion and bacon and cook for 2-3 minutes or until onion is golden. Remove from pan and set aside.
3　Melt remaining butter in pan, add flour and cook for 3-4 minutes or until a light straw color. Combine stock, wine, tomato paste and sugar. Remove pan from heat and gradually blend in stock mixture. Cook over a medium heat, stirring constantly, until sauce boils and thickens. Stir in parsley and season to taste with black pepper. Return meat mixture to pan, cover and simmer gently for 1¹/₂-2 hours or until meat is tender. Set aside to cool slightly.
4　To make crust, combine butter, sour cream and egg in a bowl. Sift in 1 cup/125 g flour and add thyme. Mix until well combined. Spread two-thirds of batter over base and sides of a shallow ovenproof dish, then spoon in meat mixture. Lightly knead remaining flour into the remaining dough. Press out on a lightly floured surface, using palm of hand, to ¹/₂ in/1 cm thick and cut into rounds using a 1¹/₄ in/3 cm metal pastry cutter. Top filling with dough rounds, overlapping them slightly. Bake for 30 minutes, or until crust is golden.

LAMB POT ROAST

Pot roasting dates back to prehistoric times when clay pots were filled with game, whole cuts of meat or poultry and vegetables, then hung over a fire to simmer. Lean meats that need long slow cooking are ideal for pot roasting.

Serves 6

- ☐ **6 tablespoons/90 g butter**
- ☐ **3-4 lb/1.5-2 kg leg of lamb**
- ☐ **14 oz/440 g canned tomatoes, mashed and undrained**
- ☐ **¹/₂ cup/125 mL red wine**
- ☐ **3 tablespoons tomato paste**
- ☐ **4 teaspoons Worcestershire sauce**
- ☐ **¹/₄ teaspoon mixed dried herbs**
- ☐ **1 teaspoon sugar**
- ☐ **freshly ground black pepper**
- ☐ **oil**
- ☐ **3 carrots, peeled and halved lengthwise**
- ☐ **3 turnips, peeled and halved lengthwise**
- ☐ **6 small onions, peeled**
- ☐ **3 large potatoes, peeled and halved**

1　Melt 2 tablespoons/30 g butter in a large heavy-based saucepan and cook meat on all sides until well browned.
2　Combine tomatoes, red wine, tomato paste, Worcestershire sauce, herbs, sugar and black pepper to taste. Pour over meat, bring to a boil, then reduce heat, cover, and simmer for 1¹/₂ hours or until meat is tender.
3　About 30 minutes before meat finishes cooking, heat oil and remaining butter in a large heavy-based skillet. Add carrots, turnips, onions and potatoes and cook until vegetables are lightly browned. Reduce heat to low and cook gently for 15-20 minutes or until vegetables are tender.
4　Remove meat from pan, place on a serving platter and set aside to keep warm. Bring sauce that remains in pan to a boil and cook for 10 minutes or until sauce reduces and thickens slightly. Serve sauce with meat and vegetables.
Cook's tip: A veal shank, a whole chicken or a piece of topside beef are also delicious cooked in this way.

ROAST PORK WITH APPLE STUFFING

Serves 6
Oven temperature 500°F/250°C

- ☐ **3 lb/1.5 kg loin of pork, with bone in and rind scored**
- ☐ **1 tablespoon salt**

APPLE STUFFING
- ☐ **2 tablespoons/30 g butter**
- ☐ **1 green apple, peeled, cored and finely chopped**
- ☐ **1 cup/60 g bread crumbs, made from stale bread**
- ☐ **1 teaspoon finely grated lemon rind**
- ☐ **1 teaspoon ground allspice**
- ☐ **4 teaspoons apple jelly**
- ☐ **¹/₄ cup golden raisins**

1　Using a sharp knife, make a pocket in the pork by separating bones from meat, leaving both ends intact.
2　To make stuffing, melt butter in a skillet and cook apple for 2-3 minutes or until soft. Remove pan from heat and stir in bread crumbs, lemon rind, allspice, apple jelly and raisins.
3　Pack mixture into pocket in pork and place on a roasting rack in a baking dish. Rub rind of pork with salt and bake for 20 minutes, reduce heat to 375°/190°C and bake for 1 hour longer or until meat is cooked through. Let stand for 10 minutes before carving.

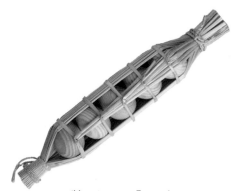

'How to wrap 5 eggs'
Rural Japanese packaging

FARMHOUSE CHICKEN CASSEROLE

Serves 4
Oven temperature 400°F/200°C

- ☐ **3 lb/1.5 kg chicken pieces**
- ☐ **¼ cup/30g seasoned flour**
- ☐ **¼ cup/60 g butter**
- ☐ **2 cloves garlic, crushed**
- ☐ **2½ cups/625 mL chicken stock**
- ☐ **3 tablespoons tomato paste**
- ☐ **4 teaspoons polyunsaturated oil**
- ☐ **1 turnip, peeled and diced**
- ☐ **2 small carrots, diced**
- ☐ **1 parsnip, peeled and diced**
- ☐ **8 small onions, peeled**
- ☐ **3 slices bacon, trimmed and chopped**
- ☐ **8 new potatoes, peeled and quartered**
- ☐ **freshly ground black pepper**
- ☐ **⅓ cup finely chopped fresh parsley**

1   Toss chicken in flour to coat. Shake off excess flour and reserve 1 tablespoon.

2   Melt butter in a large skillet and cook chicken over a medium heat until brown on all sides. Transfer to a large casserole dish.

3   Add garlic and remaining flour to pan and cook over a low heat for 1 minute. Combine stock and tomato paste. Remove pan from heat and gradually blend in stock mixture. Cook over a medium heat, stirring constantly, until mixture boils and thickens. Pour over chicken in dish. Cover and bake chicken for 30 minutes.

4   Heat oil in a large skillet and cook turnip, carrots and parsnip over a medium heat for 3-4 minutes. Remove from pan and set aside. Add onions and bacon to pan and cook for 4-5 minutes or until bacon is crisp.

5   Stir turnip, carrots, parsnip, onion mixture, potatoes, black pepper to taste and parsley into chicken mixture and bake for 40 minutes longer or until chicken is done.

Roast Pork with Apple Stuffing

ROAST TURKEY

The Spaniards brought turkeys to Europe from North America in the 1520s. Cooks soon developed wonderful dishes for special occasions with delicious stuffings and accompaniments. Try this Roast Turkey for a Christmas or Thanksgiving dinner.

Serves 10
Oven temperature 350°F/180°C

- [ ] **8 lb/4 kg turkey**
- [ ] **¹/₄ cup/60 g butter, melted**
- [ ] **1 cup/250 mL chicken stock**

VEAL FORCEMEAT

- [ ] **2 tablespoons/30 g butter**
- [ ] **1 onion, finely chopped**
- [ ] **1 slice bacon, finely chopped**
- [ ] **¹/₂ lb/250 g lean minced veal**
- [ ] **3 cups/185 g bread crumbs, made from stale bread**
- [ ] **¹/₂ teaspoon finely grated lemon rind**
- [ ] **4 teaspoons finely chopped fresh parsley**
- [ ] **¹/₂ teaspoon dried sage**
- [ ] **pinch ground nutmeg**
- [ ] **freshly ground black pepper**
- [ ] **1 egg, lightly beaten**

APPLE AND CHESTNUT STUFFING

- [ ] **14 oz/440 g canned chestnut puree, strained**
- [ ] **2 cooking apples, cored, peeled and grated**
- [ ] **3 cups/185 g bread crumbs, made from stale bread**
- [ ] **1 onion, finely chopped**
- [ ] **1 stalk celery, finely chopped**
- [ ] **¹/₃ cup finely chopped walnuts**
- [ ] **4 teaspoons finely chopped fresh parsley**
- [ ] **3 tablespoons/45 g butter, melted**
- [ ] **freshly ground black pepper**
- [ ] **pinch ground nutmeg**
- [ ] **1 egg, lightly beaten**

1   To make forcemeat, melt butter in a skillet and cook onion and bacon for 4-5 minutes or until bacon is crisp. Add veal, bread crumbs, lemon rind, parsley, sage, nutmeg, black pepper to taste and egg. Mix well to combine.

2   To make stuffing, combine chestnut puree, apples, bread crumbs, onion, celery, walnuts, parsley, butter, black pepper to taste, nutmeg and egg.

3   Remove giblets and neck from turkey. Wipe turkey inside and out and dry well. Place stuffing in body cavity and lightly fill neck end of turkey with forcemeat. Secure openings with metal skewers and truss legs and wings.

4   Place turkey on a roasting rack in a baking pan. Brush with butter, then pour chicken stock into baking pan. Bake for 3-3¹/₂ hours or until tender. Baste frequently with pan juices during cooking. Set aside to stand for 20 minutes before carving.

To make forcemeat, melt butter in a skillet and cook onion and bacon for 4-5 minutes.

Place stuffing in body cavity and lightly fill neck end of turkey with forcemeat.

Secure openings of turkey with metal skewers and truss legs and wings.

PORK WITH SAUERKRAUT

Serves 6

- ☐ **2 tablespoons/30 g butter**
- ☐ **1¹/₂ lb/750 g pork tenderloin, sliced**
- ☐ **2 onions, sliced**
- ☐ **2 green apples, cored, peeled and sliced**
- ☐ **2 teaspoons ground paprika**
- ☐ **1 teaspoon caraway seeds**
- ☐ **freshly ground black pepper**
- ☐ **³/₄ cup/185 mL chicken stock**
- ☐ **¹/₄ cup/60 mL dry white wine**
- ☐ **3 tablespoons tomato paste**
- ☐ **14 oz/440 g canned or bottled sauerkraut, drained**
- ☐ **¹/₂ cup/125 g sour cream**

1   Melt butter in a large saucepan and cook pork slices over a medium heat for 3-4 minutes each side, or until meat just changes color. Remove from pan and set aside.

2   Add onions and apples to pan and cook for 4-5 minutes or until onions soften. Stir in paprika and caraway seeds and cook over a medium heat for 1 minute. Season to taste with black pepper.

3   Combine stock, wine and tomato paste. Pour into pan and cook over a medium heat, stirring constantly to lift sediment from bottom of pan. Bring to a boil, then reduce heat and simmer for 10 minutes.

4   Return meat to pan, stir in sauerkraut and cook for 2-3 minutes. Remove pan from heat, stir in sour cream and serve immediately.

SAUERKRAUT

To make sauerkraut, you will require about 6 lb/3 kg cabbage. Trim cabbage, cut into quarters, remove core, and finely shred. Place in a large bowl, sprinkle with ¹/₄ cup salt, mix to combine. Set aside until cabbage wilts. Pack firmly into a sterilized wide-mouthed 1 gallon/4 liter crock or glass jar. Cover surface of cabbage with clean muslin cloth. Choose a china or glass saucer or plate that fits snugly into the top of the container, place on top of muslin and weight heavily. Place in a warm place – around 70°F/21°C is ideal.

As the cabbage ferments bubbles and scum rise to the surface. Each day rinse weight, plate and muslin in warm water. Remove any scum and replace muslin, plate and weight. Fermentation takes 2-4 weeks. Store in glass jars, covered with the brine.

BOILED BEEF DINNER

*Simple and satisfying,
this Boiled Beef Dinner is served
with creamy mashed potatoes and
horseradish cream. There are sure
to be requests for second helpings.*

Serves 6

- ☐ 3 lb/1.5 kg corned beef
- ☐ 2-3 tablespoons brown sugar
- ☐ 4 teaspoons cider vinegar
- ☐ 2 sprigs fresh mint
- ☐ 1 onion, peeled and studded
  with 4 whole cloves
- ☐ 6 peppercorns
- ☐ 6 small carrots, peeled
- ☐ 6 small onions, peeled
- ☐ 3 parsnips, peeled and halved

REDCURRANT GLAZE
- ☐ $1/2$ cup (155 g) redcurrant jelly
- ☐ 3 tablespoons orange juice
- ☐ 4 teaspoons Grand Marnier

1   Place meat in a large heavy-based saucepan. Add brown sugar, vinegar, mint, onion, peppercorns and enough water to cover meat. Bring to a boil, then reduce heat and simmer for $1^1/4$-$1^1/2$ hours.
2   Add carrots, onions and parsnips to pan and cook over a low heat for 40 minutes longer or until vegetables are tender.
3   To make glaze, place redcurrant jelly, orange juice and Grand Marnier in a small saucepan and cook over a low heat, stirring occasionally, until well blended. Transfer meat to a serving plate and brush with redcurrant mixture. Slice meat and serve with vegetables and any remaining redcurrant mixture.
Cook's tip: To make horseradish cream, whip $1/2$ cup/125 mL heavy cream until soft peaks form then fold through $1/4$ cup prepared horseradish.

Pork with Sauerkraut, Boiled Beef Dinner

MARINATED RABBIT IN RED WINE SAUCE

Serves 6
Oven temperature 350°F/180°C

- ☐ 3 x 2 lb/1 kg rabbits, cleaned and quartered
- ☐ ¹/₄ cup/60 g butter
- ☐ 2 tablespoons olive oil
- ☐ 6 slices bacon, chopped
- ☐ 12 pearl onions, peeled
- ☐ ¹/₄ cup/30 g flour
- ☐ 3 cups/750 mL chicken stock
- ☐ ¹/₄ cup/60 mL port
- ☐ 2-3 tablespoons Dijon mustard
- ☐ ¹/₄ cup/60 mL tomato paste
- ☐ ¹/₂ lb/250 g button mushrooms
- ☐ 14 oz/440 g canned butter beans
- ☐ 2 bay leaves
- ☐ 4 teaspoons chopped fresh oregano

RED WINE MARINADE
- ☐ 1 large carrot, diced
- ☐ 2 stalks celery, sliced
- ☐ 1 large onion, sliced
- ☐ 3 bay leaves
- ☐ 2 cloves garlic, crushed
- ☐ 4 whole cloves
- ☐ 4 teaspoons finely chopped fresh tarragon
- ☐ 4 teaspoons finely chopped fresh parsley
- ☐ ¹/₂ cup/125 mL olive oil
- ☐ red wine

1 To make marinade, place carrot, celery, onion, bay leaves, garlic, cloves, tarragon, parsley and oil in a large glass or ceramic bowl. Add rabbit and enough red wine to cover mixture. Cover and marinate overnight in the refrigerator. Strain marinade into a clean bowl and reserve. Discard vegetables.

2 Melt 2 tablespoons/30 g butter with oil in a large deep baking pan. Add rabbit and bake for 20-25 minutes or until lightly browned. Remove rabbit from pan and set aside to keep warm. Place baking pan with pan juices over a high heat. Stir in bacon and onions and cook for 4-5 minutes or until onions are golden. Remove from pan and set aside.

3 Melt remaining butter in pan, stir in flour and cook over a medium heat until dark brown, taking care not to burn. Combine 3 cups (750 mL) reserved marinade, chicken stock and port. Remove pan from heat and gradually blend in marinade mixture. Cook over a medium heat, stirring constantly, until sauce boils and thickens.

4 Reduce heat and whisk in mustard and tomato paste. Return rabbit, bacon and onions to pan and bake for 30 minutes. Stir in mushrooms, beans, bay leaves and oregano. Season to taste with black pepper and bake for 30 minutes longer, or until rabbit is tender.

LAMB AND VEGETABLE STEW

Serves 6

- ☐ 1¹/₂ lb/750 g leg lamb, cut in 1 in/2 cm cubes
- ☐ 3 tablespoons seasoned flour
- ☐ 1 tablespoon/15 g butter
- ☐ 2 tablespoons oil
- ☐ 6 pearl onions, peeled and bases left intact
- ☐ 6 small new potatoes, scrubbed
- ☐ 2 cloves garlic, crushed
- ☐ 3 stalks celery, sliced
- ☐ 1 red pepper, sliced
- ☐ 2 slices bacon, chopped
- ☐ 1 carrot, sliced
- ☐ 1¹/₂ cups/375 mL beef stock
- ☐ ¹/₂ cup/125 mL red wine
- ☐ 1 tablespoon tomato paste
- ☐ 2-3 tablespoons finely chopped fresh rosemary
- ☐ ¹/₂ lb/250 g green beans, trimmed and cut into 1 in/2.5 cm lengths
- ☐ freshly ground black pepper
- ☐ 4 teaspoons corn starch blended with 2 tablespoons water

1 Toss meat in flour. Heat butter and 1 tablespoon oil in a large heavy-based saucepan and cook meat in batches until brown on all sides. Remove from pan and set aside.

2 Heat remaining oil in pan and cook onions and potatoes until brown on all sides. Remove from pan and set aside. Add garlic, celery, red pepper and bacon and cook for 4-5 minutes. Return meat, onions and potatoes to pan. Mix in carrot, stock, wine, tomato paste and rosemary, bring to a boil, then reduce heat and simmer, covered, for 1 hour or until meat is tender. Stir in beans and corn starch mixture, season to taste with black pepper and cook for 10 minutes longer.

Lamb and Vegetable Stew, Marinated Rabbit in Red Wine Sauce

meaty MATTERS

There are many different ways of cooking meat. The method you choose will depend on the cut you wish to cook.

Dry heat roasting: First sauté the meat to brown, then oven-bake at a high temperature for a short time. This method of cooking is ideal for those who enjoy meat browned on the outside and rare in the center. The more tender cuts of meat should be used for this method.

Pot roasting: The more economical cuts of meat that would be tough if dry roasted are used for this method of cooking. First sauté the meat over a medium-high heat to brown, then transfer to a covered roasting dish and cook slowly in the oven, or simmer in a covered, large, deep heavy-based saucepan on top of stove. In both cases the lid must fit tightly. A small quantity of liquid and vegetables can be added if you wish and basting is not required.

Stewing meat: This method of cooking meat is most suitable for those cuts of meat that require long slow cooking to tenderize them. Trim meat of all visible fat and cut into evenly sized cubes. Brown meat in batches, either in the pan that you are going to cook the stew in, or in a skillet, then transfer to a large saucepan. Toss meat in flour, then add vegetables, flavorings and stock, water or red wine to pan, cover and bring to a boil, then reduce heat and simmer for 1¹/₂-2 hours or until meat is tender. This gives what is known as a brown stew. If making a white stew, do not brown meat before cooking and use light ingredients such as veal stock, water or white wine.

harvest FESTIVAL

Vegetables, grains, eggs and cheese

Vegetables, rice and grains, eggs and cheese are among the oldest foods known to man. In fact, cheesemaking has been known since ancient times. In Tudor days a large household could consume as much as seventy kilograms of cheese in a week.

Top: Wheat weaving 'Norfolk Lantern'
Right: Mushroom Gougere (page 26),
Wholemeal Spinach Quiche (page 26),
Spinach and Basil Risotto (page 27)

POTATOES WITH RED PEPPER AND BACON

Crisp golden slices of potato baked with onions, red peppers and bacon are a meal in themselves when served with a crisp green salad.

Serves 8
Oven temperature 400°F/200°C

- ☐ **8 potatoes, peeled and cut into ³/₈ in/1 cm thick slices**
- ☐ **4 red onions, cut into eighths**
- ☐ **6 large red peppers, cut into long strips, 1 in/2.5 cm wide**
- ☐ **1 lb/500 g bacon, cut into ³/₈ in/1 cm strips**
- ☐ **2 teaspoons finely chopped fresh rosemary**
- ☐ **4 teaspoons chopped fresh parsley**
- ☐ **1 clove garlic, crushed**
- ☐ **freshly ground black pepper**
- ☐ **2-3 tablespoons olive oil**

1 Place potatoes, onions, red peppers and bacon in a large bowl. Stir in rosemary, parsley and garlic. Season to taste with black pepper. Add oil and toss to coat all ingredients.
2 Spoon mixture into a lightly greased, large ovenproof dish and bake for 55-60 minutes, or until potatoes are done, golden and crisp.

WHOLEMEAL SPINACH QUICHE

Serves 6
Oven temperature 425°F/220°C

- ☐ **1 cup/155 g whole wheat flour, sifted and chaff returned**
- ☐ **2²/₃ tablespoons oil**
- ☐ **1 egg, lightly beaten**
- ☐ **4 teaspoons iced water**

SPINACH FILLING
- ☐ **2 tablespoons/30 g butter**
- ☐ **1 onion, finely chopped**
- ☐ **¹/₂ bunch spinach, stalks removed and leaves finely shredded**
- ☐ **3 eggs, lightly beaten**
- ☐ **1¹/₄ cups/300 g sour cream**
- ☐ **pinch ground nutmeg**
- ☐ **freshly ground black pepper**
- ☐ **¹/₂ cup/60 g grated sharp cheese (such as cheddar)**

1 Place flour in a large mixing bowl. Combine oil, egg and water, add to flour and mix to a firm dough. Turn dough onto a floured surface and knead lightly. Cover and refrigerate for 30 minutes.
2 Roll out pastry place in a lightly greased 9 in/23 cm tart pan. Trim edges and line with wax paper. Fill with dried beans or rice and bake blind for 15 minutes. Remove beans and paper and bake for 10 minutes longer. Remove from oven and set aside to cool slightly.
3 To make filling, melt butter in a skillet and cook onion over a medium heat for 4-5 minutes or until soft. Stir in spinach and cook for 2-3 minutes or until spinach wilts. Remove pan from heat and set aside.
4 Combine eggs, sour cream, nutmeg, black pepper to taste and cheese. Spread spinach mixture over pastry base, then carefully spoon in egg mixture. Reduce temperature to 350°F/180°C and bake for 30 minutes or until firm.

MUSHROOM GOUGERE

Serves 4
Oven temperature 400°F/200°C

CHOUX PASTRY
- ☐ **1 cup/250 mL water**
- ☐ **6 tablespoons/90 g butter**
- ☐ **1 cup/125 g flour, sifted**
- ☐ **4 eggs**

MUSHROOM FILLING
- ☐ **5 oz/155 g button mushrooms, sliced**
- ☐ **3 eggs, lightly beaten**
- ☐ **¹/₄ cup/155 g sour cream**
- ☐ **¹/₂ cup/125 mL heavy cream**
- ☐ **4 teaspoons flour**
- ☐ **1 cup/125 g grated sharp cheese (such as cheddar)**
- ☐ **4 teaspoons chopped fresh parsley**
- ☐ **freshly ground black pepper**
- ☐ **pinch ground nutmeg**

1 To make pastry, place water and butter in a saucepan. Cover and cook over a medium heat until butter melts and mixture just boils. Remove pan from heat and add flour all at once. Stir vigorously with a wooden spoon, over a low heat, until mixture forms a ball and pulls away from sides of pan. Set aside to cool slightly.
2 Add eggs one at a time, beating well after each addition until mixture is smooth and glossy. Spread mixture around sides of a greased shallow ovenproof dish.

3 To make filling, combine mushrooms, eggs, sour cream, cream, flour, cheese and parsley. Season to taste with black pepper and nutmeg. Spoon filling into center of pastry and bake for 35-40 minutes or until filling is firm and pastry is puffed and golden.

SPINACH AND BASIL RISOTTO

Risotto is an Italian favorite. Wonderful as a first course, main course or an accompaniment to meat, fish or poultry, it is nutritious and easy to make.

Serves 4

- ☐ **1 bunch spinach, stalks removed and leaves chopped**
- ☐ **1 cup/250 mL water**
- ☐ **$^1/_4$ cup/60 g butter**
- ☐ **1 large onion, finely chopped**
- ☐ **2 cloves garlic, crushed**
- ☐ **2 cups/440 g brown rice**
- ☐ **$^1/_2$ cup/125 mL white wine**
- ☐ **5 cups/1.25 liters hot chicken stock**
- ☐ **5 tablespoons pine nuts, toasted**
- ☐ **$^1/_2$ cup/30 g fresh basil leaves**
- ☐ **2-3 tablespoons olive oil**

1 Place spinach and water in a saucepan and cook over a medium heat for 1-2 minutes. Bring to a boil and cook for 1 minute or until spinach is tender. Remove from heat and set aside to cool.

2 Place spinach mixture in a food processor or blender and process until smooth. Set aside.

3 Melt butter in a saucepan and cook onion and garlic for 4-5 minutes or until onion is soft. Add rice to pan and stir to coat with butter mixture. Pour in wine and half the chicken stock. Cook over a medium heat, stirring occasionally until almost all the liquid is absorbed. Stir in remaining stock with reserved spinach mixture and cook until almost all the liquid is absorbed.

4 Place 4 tablespoons pine nuts, basil and oil in a food processor or blender and process until smooth. Stir into rice mixture. Sprinkle with remaining pine nuts and serve immediately.

WHEAT WEAVING

Straw has been used as a functional and decorative fiber by man for thousands of years. Functionally it has been used in the cottage industry for thatching, making baskets, beehives, hats, handbags and furniture.

Wheat weavings are one of the decorative ways in which straw is used. These traditional symbols of prosperity have been an important part of harvest customs wherever cereals are grown. They no longer carry the ritual significance that they once did, but are today enjoyed as a creative and decorative art form in their own right.

Enjoy the ones in this book and may they bring you prosperity too.

'Miss Dorothy'

Potatoes with Red Pepper and Bacon

PUMPKIN GNOCCHI WITH ZUCCHINI SAUCE

Thursday is gnocchi day in Rome, when good cooks use their old potatoes to make gnocchi. This version made with pumpkin and served with a vegetable sauce, is a variation of the traditional Roman version, but just as delicious.

Serves 6

- ☐ **2 tablespoons/30 g butter**
- ☐ **1 onion, finely chopped**
- ☐ **2 cloves garlic, crushed**
- ☐ **1^1/4 lb/600 g pumpkin, peeled and finely grated**
- ☐ **8 oz/250 g ricotta cheese**
- ☐ **^{1}/2 cup/60 g grated fresh Parmesan cheese**
- ☐ **3 tablespoons flour**
- ☐ **1 egg yolk, lightly beaten**
- ☐ **^{1}/4 teaspoon ground nutmeg**
- ☐ **flour**

ZUCCHINI SAUCE
- ☐ **2-3 tablespoons olive oil**
- ☐ **3 large zucchini, sliced**
- ☐ **5 scallions, chopped**
- ☐ **^{3}/4 cup/185 mL cream**
- ☐ **freshly ground black pepper**
- ☐ **^{1}/4 cup/60 g butter, melted**
- ☐ **^{1}/2 cup/60 g grated fresh Parmesan cheese**
- ☐ **ground nutmeg**

1   Melt butter in a small saucepan and cook onion and garlic for 4-5 minutes or until onion is soft. Remove pan from heat and transfer onion mixture to a large mixing bowl. Add pumpkin, ricotta cheese, Parmesan cheese, flour, egg yolk and nutmeg. Season to taste with black pepper and mix to combine.

2   Form small spoonfuls of mixture into egg shapes. Toss in flour to coat, shake off excess and refrigerate until firm. Cook gnocchi a few at a time in boiling water in a large saucepan until they rise to the surface. Remove from pan using a slotted spoon and set aside to keep warm.

3   To make sauce, heat oil in a saucepan and cook zucchini and scallions for 4-5 minutes or until soft. Set aside to cool. Transfer mixture to a food processor or blender and process until smooth.

Place in a clean saucepan, stir in cream and season to taste with black pepper. Cook sauce over a low heat until it is almost boiling.

4   Spoon Zucchini Sauce into base of serving dish, top with gnocchi, pour melted butter over, sprinkle with Parmesan cheese and dust with nutmeg. Serve immediately.

Add pumpkin, ricotta cheese, Parmesan cheese, flour, egg yolk and nutmeg to onion mixture and mix to combine.

Form small spoonfuls of mixture into egg shapes. Toss in flour to coat, shake off excess and refrigerate until firm.

Cook gnocchi in boiling water in a large saucepan until they rise to the surface.

PASTA WITH SPINACH TERRINE

Wrap some pasta and vegetables in prosciutto or ham for this 'feast for the eyes'. Great for a picnic or luncheon served with a crisp green salad and crusty bread.

Serves 8
Oven temperature 350°F/180°C

- ☐ **2 tablespoons/30 g butter**
- ☐ **1 large onion, finely chopped**
- ☐ **2 cloves garlic, crushed**
- ☐ **8 oz/250 g spinach fettuccine**
- ☐ **8 oz/250 g ricotta cheese**
- ☐ **$^1/_2$ cup/125 g sour cream**
- ☐ **$^1/_3$ cup grated fresh Parmesan cheese**
- ☐ **8 oz/250 g frozen spinach, thawed, drained and pureed**
- ☐ **5 eggs, lightly beaten**
- ☐ **$1^1/_2$ oz/45 g pine nuts, toasted and chopped**
- ☐ **$^1/_4$ cup coarsely chopped fresh basil**
- ☐ **freshly ground black pepper**
- ☐ **12 slices prosciutto or ham**

1   Melt butter in a skillet and cook onion and garlic over a low heat for 4-5 minutes or until onion is soft. Remove from heat and set aside.

2   Cook fettuccine in boiling water in a large saucepan, following package directions. Drain, rinse under cold running water and set aside.

3   Place ricotta cheese, sour cream, reserved onion mixture, Parmesan cheese, spinach, eggs, pine nuts and basil in a food processor or blender and process until smooth. Season to taste with black pepper.

4   Chop fettuccine roughly and mix with cream mixture. Spoon into an oiled and lined 5 x 9 in/12 x 23 cm loaf pan. Cover with aluminium foil and place in a baking dish with enough water to come halfway up the sides of pan. Bake for 35-40 minutes or until firm.

5   Cool terrine in pan for 10 minutes, then turn out and set aside to cool completely. Wrap prosciutto or ham slices around terrine to completely encase. Serve cut into slices.

Layered Leek and Potato Gratin, Pasta with Spinach Terrine, Vegetable Croquettes

Wooden boad and plates Country Furniture Antiques Plants Liquidamber Nursery

LAYERED LEEK AND POTATO GRATIN

Serves 4
Oven temperature 350°F/180°C

- [ ] **2 tablespoons/30 g butter**
- [ ] **1 large clove garlic, crushed**
- [ ] **4 large potatoes, peeled and cooked until just tender**
- [ ] **4 leeks, sliced**
- [ ] **³/4 cup/185 mL cream**
- [ ] **¹/4 cup raisins, chopped**
- [ ] **3 oz/90 g Jarlsberg cheese, grated**

1 Combine butter and garlic, then rub over base and sides of a shallow oven-proof dish. Set aside.
2 Cut potatoes into thin slices and arrange in a layer over base of dish. Top with a layer of leeks. Repeat with remaining potatoes and leeks, finishing with a layer of leeks.
3 Pour cream over potato mixture in dish, then sprinkle with raisins and cheese. Bake for 30-35 minutes or until golden and cooked through.

VEGETABLE CROQUETTES

Serves 4

- [ ] **2 cups/500 g cold cooked vegetables, such as potatoes, pumpkin, peas, beans and sweet potato**
- [ ] **1 egg, lightly beaten**
- [ ] **¹/2 cup/30 g bread crumbs, made from stale bread**
- [ ] **¹/2 teaspoon ground cumin**
- [ ] **¹/2 teaspoon ground coriander**
- [ ] **4 teaspoons chopped fresh mint**
- [ ] **freshly ground black pepper**
- [ ] **³/4 cup/90 g toasted bread crumbs**
- [ ] **2-3 tablespoons olive oil**

1 Place vegetables in a mixing bowl and mash with the back of a fork. Add egg, bread crumbs, cumin, coriander, mint and black pepper to taste.
2 Divide mixture into eight portions and shape into patties using floured hands. Press patties into dried bread crumbs and refrigerate for 30 minutes. Heat oil in a heavy-based skillet and cook patties for 3-4 minutes each side or until golden. Drain on absorbent kitchen paper and serve immediately.

vegetable PERFECTION

Make the most of garden fresh vegetables with these preparation and cooking tips.

Ready: Easy cooking and preparation depends on having good basic equipment. It is worth investing a little money in equipment, such as a large chopping board, a small sharp vegetable or paring knife as well as several larger sharp knives for cutting and chopping, a grater, a vegetable peeler and a colander or large sieve. Sharp knives make preparation a breeze.

Set: Wash vegetables before preparing, but do not soak them. Soaking draws out the water soluble vitamins and your vegetables will have a lower nutrient content. As with every rule there are exceptions and it may be necessary to soak very dirty vegetables to remove dirt and insects. Always keep soaking time to a minimum.

Whole vegetables with skins on have a higher nutrient and fiber content than finely chopped and peeled vegetables. Many of the vitamins and minerals are stored just under the skin. Only peel vegetables if necessary. For maximum nutritional value, prepare vegetables just before cooking and serve as soon as they are cooked.

Go: Here's how to cube, dice, mince, grate and slice.
Cube: cut vegetable into about ³/8 in/1 cm pieces.
Dice: cut vegetable into about ¹/4 in/5 mm pieces.
Mince: cut vegetable into about ¹/8 in/3 mm pieces.
Grate: use either a hand grater or a food processor with a grating attachment.
Slice: cut very thin to thick. You can also slice diagonally or into rings.

Dresser Country Furniture Antiques *Preserving pan* Country Store Antiques

the pantry SHELF

Jams, pickles and chutneys

*I*n the seventeenth century when sugar was first plentiful, fruit preserving became popular. Delicious preserves such as Pickled Onions and Strawberry Jam will add that homemade touch to your pantry, or make lovely gifts for special friends.

Top: Wheat weaving 'Corazon de Trigo'
Left: Top shelf; Spicy Apple Chutney,
Cinnamon Pears in Brandy, Corn and
Mustard Seed Relish
Bottom shelf; Pickled Dill Cucumbers,
Pickled Onions (all recipes page 34)

CINNAMON PEARS
IN BRANDY

Makes 3.5-4 quarts/liters

- [ ] **8 small pears, peeled, halved and cored with stems left intact**
- [ ] **¹/₄ cup/60 mL lemon juice**
- [ ] **1 cup/250 g sugar**
- [ ] **1¹/₂ cups/375 mL water, plus additional to cover pears**
- [ ] **1 cinnamon stick, broken into pieces**
- [ ] **2 teaspoons grated lime rind**
- [ ] **3 cups/750 mL brandy**

1 Core pears and place in a large bowl, pour over lemon juice and just enough water to cover pears.

2 Place sugar and water in a large heavy-based saucepan and cook over a low heat, stirring until sugar dissolves. Bring to a boil without stirring.

3 Drain pears and add to pan with cinnamon stick and lime rind. Cook over a low heat until pears are just tender.

4 Arrange pears in hot sterilized jars. Stir brandy into sugar syrup, then pour over pears to completely cover. Seal and store in a cool dark place.

PICKLED DILL
CUCUMBERS

Makes 5-6 quarts/liters

- [ ] **6 lb/3 kg gherkins or small pickling cucumbers, trimmed**
- [ ] **salt**
- [ ] **10 cups/2.5 litres white wine vinegar**
- [ ] **4 teaspoons black mustard seeds**
- [ ] **¹/₂ teaspoon whole black peppercorns**
- [ ] **4 whole cloves**
- [ ] **4 sprigs fresh dill**

1 Place gherkins or cucumbers on sheets of paper towels and sprinkle with salt. Set aside to stand for 2-3 hours. Rinse under cold running water and pat dry on paper towels. Place gherkins or cucumbers in a heatproof bowl.

2 Place vinegar, mustard seeds, peppercorns, cloves and dill in a large saucepan and bring to a boil. Pour mixture over gherkins or cucumbers in bowl and set aside to stand overnight.

3 Remove cloves. Place gherkins or cucumbers and liquid in a large saucepan and cook over a medium heat until gherkins or cucumbers are just tender. Remove pan from heat and set aside to cool. Pack gherkins or cucumbers and liquid into hot sterilized jars. Seal and store in a cool dark place.

PICKLED ONIONS

Makes 4 quarts/liters

- [ ] **4 lb/2 kg pickling onions, unpeeled**
- [ ] **24 oz/750 g salt**

PICKLING VINEGAR
- [ ] **6 cups/1.5 liters white wine vinegar**
- [ ] **4 teaspoons salt**
- [ ] **2 teaspoons ground ginger**
- [ ] **6 whole cloves**
- [ ] **2 red chilies, cut in half**
- [ ] **2 teaspoons yellow mustard seeds**
- [ ] **6 whole black peppercorns**
- [ ] **2 bay leaves**

1 Place onions and salt in a bowl. Add enough water to cover onions and set aside to stand for 2 days. Stir occasionally during standing time.

2 Drain onions and discard liquid. Peel onions and cover with boiling water. Set aside to stand for 3 minutes, then drain and repeat twice more using additional boiling water. Pack onions into hot sterilized jars and set aside.

3 To make vinegar, place white wine vinegar, salt, ginger, cloves, chilies, mustard seeds, peppercorns and bay leaves in a large saucepan. Bring to a boil, then reduce heat and simmer for 10 minutes. Cool slightly, then pour liquid over onions in jars and seal. Store in a cool dark place for 2 months before using.

SPICY APPLE CHUTNEY

Makes 2 cups/600 g

- [ ] **2-3 tablespoons vegetable oil**
- [ ] **1 clove garlic, crushed**
- [ ] **1 teaspoon grated fresh ginger**
- [ ] **2 fresh chilies, seeded and chopped**
- [ ] **2²/₃ tablespoons mustard seeds**
- [ ] **1 teaspoon mixed spice**
- [ ] **1 teaspoon ground turmeric**
- [ ] **15 black peppercorns**
- [ ] **2 teaspoons ground cumin**
- [ ] **8 large cooking apples, cored, peeled and sliced**
- [ ] **²/₃ cup/170 mL white vinegar**
- [ ] **¹/₂ cup/125 g sugar**

1 Heat oil in a large saucepan and cook garlic, ginger and chilies over a medium heat for 2-3 minutes. Combine mustard seeds, mixed spice, turmeric, peppercorns and cumin, add to pan and cook for 3-4 minutes longer.

2 Add apples, vinegar and sugar to pan and simmer, uncovered, for 1 hour or until thick. Pour chutney into hot sterilized jars and seal when cold.

CORN AND
MUSTARD SEED RELISH

Makes 6 cups/1.5 kg

- [ ] **1 large onion, finely chopped**
- [ ] **2 cups/500 mL white wine vinegar**
- [ ] **¹/₂ cup/100 g superfine sugar**
- [ ] **4 teaspoons curry powder**
- [ ] **1 teaspoon ground turmeric**
- [ ] **2 teaspoons yellow mustard seeds**
- [ ] **2²/₃ tablespoons grated fresh ginger**
- [ ] **2 x 14 oz/440 g canned sweet corn kernels, drained**
- [ ] **1 carrot, peeled and finely chopped**
- [ ] **2 stalks celery, chopped**
- [ ] **1 red pepper, chopped**
- [ ] **2 tablespoons corn starch, blended with 5 tablespoons water**
- [ ] **freshly ground black pepper**

1 Place onion in a saucepan and add enough water to cover onion. Bring to a boil, remove from heat, drain and set aside.

2 Place vinegar, sugar, curry powder, turmeric, mustard seeds and ginger in a clean saucepan. Bring to a boil, then reduce heat and simmer for 3-4 minutes.

3 Add sweet corn kernels, carrot, celery, red pepper and onion to pan. Bring to a boil, then reduce heat and simmer for 15 minutes.

4 Stir in corn starch mixture and cook over a medium heat, stirring constantly, for 5 minutes or until mixture boils and thickens. Season to taste with black pepper. Spoon relish into hot sterilized jars. Seal when cool and store in a cool dark place.

THREE-FRUIT MARMALADE

The name 'marmalade' comes from the Portuguese word for quince. The original marmalade was a quince jelly from Portugal that was taken to England in the fourteenth century. By the eighteenth century marmalade included citrus fruit, especially oranges, and had become a solid conserve that could be eaten on its own or as an accompaniment to other dishes.

Makes 6 cups/1.5 kg

- ☐ **2 large oranges**
- ☐ **2 limes**
- ☐ **1 large grapefruit**
- ☐ **4 cups/1 liter water**
- ☐ **7 cups/1.75 kg sugar**

1 Cut oranges, limes and grapefruit in half, then slice thinly, discarding seeds. Place fruit in a large bowl and pour over water. Cover and stand overnight.

2 Transfer fruit and water to a large saucepan and bring to a boil, then reduce heat and simmer, uncovered, for 1 hour or until fruit is soft.

3 Add sugar, stirring constantly without boiling, until sugar dissolves. Bring to a boil and cook, uncovered, without stirring, for 45 minutes or until marmalade gels when tested.

4 Let stand 10 minutes before pouring marmalade into hot sterilized jars. Seal when cold.

MIXED-BERRY JAM

Makes 4 cups/1 kg

- ☐ **1¹/₂ lb/800 g mixed fresh berries**
- ☐ **1 cup/250 mL water**
- ☐ **1¹/₂ lb/800 g sugar**
- ☐ **¹/₄ cup/60 mL lemon juice**

1 Place berries, water, sugar and lemon juice in a large saucepan and cook over a low heat, stirring until sugar dissolves.

2 Bring to a boil, then reduce heat and simmer for 30-35 minutes or until jam gels when tested.

3 Let stand for 10 minutes, then pour into hot sterilized jars. Seal when cold.

CANNING FRUIT

Canned fruit is a delicious addition to any pantry and will bring the taste of summer to winter meals. It is a good way of preserving an excess of fruit and you can make gourmet preserves such as Cinnamon Pears in Brandy.

There are a number of methods you can use for preserving fruit. The quick-water bath method is the quickest and easiest.

Quick-water bath method: You will require a large saucepan, a rack that fits inside the saucepan to stand the jars on, and a thermometer.

🍃 Make a sugar syrup before you prepare and pack the fruit. You will need about ³/₄ cup/185 mL for each 1 pint/600 mL jar. Use granulated not superfine sugar for the syrup.

🍃 To make a medium syrup, place 2 cups/500 g sugar and 3 cups/750 mL water in a saucepan and cook over a gentle heat until sugar is dissolved and syrup hot. This will give you about 2¹/₂ cups/625 mL of syrup — increase or decrease quantity as required.

🍃 Choose good quality fruit and prepare.

🍃 Pack fruit into jars. The jars should be as full as possible, as shrinkage will occur during processing.

🍃 Pour hot sugar syrup over fruit. The jars should be filled to the brim with the liquid. Twist the jars from side to side to remove any air bubbles.

🍃 Position lids on jars and screw down bands loosely.

🍃 Place jars in a saucepan on a rack and pour over warm water 100°F/38°C. The jars should be completely immersed in the water. Bring water to simmering in 25-30 minutes and simmer for 15-30 minutes depending on the fruit (see chart).

🍃 On completion of processing, remove jars from water-bath, using tongs. Tighten bands.

🍃 Set aside to cool for 24 hours.

🍃 Test for seal. Remove bands from jars and lift the jars carefully by the lids. If the lids are tight and secure, the seal is complete.

PROCESSING TIMES FOR FRUITS USING QUICK-WATER BATH METHOD

Apricots, whole	Remove stalks and wash	15 minutes
Apricots, halved	Cut around stone and twist halves apart	15 minutes
Peaches	Blanch for 30 seconds, place in cold water and remove skin. Halve and remove stone	30 minutes
Pears, dessert	Peel, halve and core	30 minutes
Plums, whole	Remove stalks and wash	15 minutes
Plums, halved	As for apricots	15 minutes

'How to wrap 5 eggs'
Rural Japanese packaging

jam MAKING

The following equipment is all that is needed for jam making.

A large heavy-based pan: The jam should only half-fill the pan so that it does not boil over during cooking. A wide pan will ensure fast evaporation. Pans made from aluminium, enamel on iron, or stainless steel are the best.

A large wooden spoon: For stirring the jam.

A set of kitchen scales: For weighing ingredients.

A candy thermometer: Helpful for testing the gelling point.

Jam-making instructions

᪥ Cook fruit gently with water and an acid ingredient such as lemon juice, if required.

᪥ Heat sugar in a heatproof bowl in oven at 300°F/150°C for 10 minutes before adding to fruit. Heating sugar saves time as it dissolves more quickly and does not cool the cooked fruit.

᪥ Add sugar to softened fruit and cook gently until sugar is completely dissolved.

᪥ Once sugar is dissolved bring quickly to a boil and boil rapidly until gelling point is reached.

᪥ Pour hot jam into hot sterilized jars. Cool conserves and marmalades slightly before pouring into jars, then stir gently to evenly distribute the fruit.

Sealing and storing

The jars should be sealed immediately after filling.

PLUM JAM

This jam is delicious as a cake or tart filling.

Makes 5 cups/1.2 kg

- ☐ **2 lb/1 kg plums, halved and stones removed**
- ☐ **1 cup/250 mL water**
- ☐ **4 cups/1 kg sugar**
- ☐ **1 tablespoon/15 g butter**

1 Place plums and water in a large saucepan. Bring to the boil, then reduce heat, cover and simmer for 15-20 minutes or until fruit is soft and pulpy.
2 Add sugar to pan, stirring constantly, without boiling, until sugar dissolves. Bring to a boil and cook, uncovered, for 20-30 minutes or until jam gels when tested. Stir in butter.
3 Let stand for 10 minutes, before pouring jam into hot sterilized jars. Seal immediately.

STRAWBERRY JAM

Makes 4 cups/1 kg

- ☐ **2 lb/1 kg strawberries, washed and hulled**
- ☐ **4 cups/1 kg sugar**
- ☐ **1/2 cup/125 mL lemon juice**
- ☐ **3/4 cup/185 mL water**

1 Combine strawberries, sugar, lemon juice and water in a large saucepan and cook over a low heat, stirring until sugar dissolves.
2 Bring to a boil and cook, without stirring, for about 40-45 minutes or until jam gels when tested.
3 Pour jam into hot sterilized jars. Seal immediately.

LEMON CURD

Lemon curd, butter or honey seems to have originated from the curd tarts, known as cheesecakes, of the seventeenth century.

Makes 1 cup/250 g

- ☐ **2 eggs**
- ☐ **1/2 cup/125 g sugar**
- ☐ **7 tablespoons lemon juice**
- ☐ **4 teaspoons grated lemon rind**
- ☐ **2 tablespoons/30 g butter**

1 Place eggs and sugar in a heatproof bowl and beat lightly. Stir in lemon juice, lemon rind and butter.
2 Cook in a heatproof bowl over a saucepan of simmering water for 15 minutes, stirring constantly, or until mixture thickens.
3 Pour into hot sterilized jars. Seal immediately.

GET THE SET RIGHT

You will find that some jams set (or gel) better than others. The quality of the gel depends on the balance of pectin, acid and sugar – these are all found in the fruit that you use for jam making. Adding lemon juice or commercial pectin to poor-gelling fruits will help give a better set.

Test jam when it has reduced to about half the original quantity of the mixture. Remove jam from heat and allow the bubbles to subside. Drop a spoonful onto a chilled saucer and set aside at room temperature to cool. The jam should form a skin that will wrinkle when pushed with your finger. If the jam does not pass the gelling test return to heat and boil for a few minutes longer, then retest. Remember to remove the jam from heat while testing.

Easy gel: Apples, blackcurrants, plums, damsons, gooseberries and redcurrants.
Medium gel: Apricots, blackberries, raspberries and loganberries.
Poor gel: Cherries and strawberries.

Clockwise from top right:
Milk Bread (page 41), Lemon Curd, Mixed-Berry Jam (page 35), Plum Jam, Three-Fruit Marmalade (page 35), Strawberry Jam

country
KITCHEN

Loaves, rolls and scones

*B*read has been the 'staff of life' for over
8000 years. You will never tire of the feeling
of satisfaction when you lift a loaf of
golden-brown bread from the oven. In this
chapter you will see how easy it is to bake a
variety of breads, including recipes for a
Whole Wheat Cottage Loaf, Spicy Coconut
Apple Twists and a Pecan Fruit Loaf.

Top: Wheat weaving 'Sweetheart'
Right: Herb Onion Loaves (page 40),
Hazelnut Bread (page 40), Whole Wheat
Rolls (page 40), Whole Wheat Cottage Loaf
(page 40), Milk Bread (page 41)

HERB ONION LOAVES

Herbs have been used to add flavor to food for over 5000 years.

Makes 2 loaves
Oven temperature 400°F/200°C

- ☐ 1¹/₂ oz/45 g fresh yeast
- ☐ ¹/₄ cup/60 mL lukewarm water
- ☐ 3 cups/375 g flour, sifted
- ☐ 3 cups/470 g whole wheat flour, sifted and chaff returned
- ☐ 4 teaspoons sugar
- ☐ 2 teaspoons salt
- ☐ 3 tablespoons chopped mixed fresh herbs, such as parsley, chives, rosemary and thyme
- ☐ 3 tablespoons onion flakes
- ☐ freshly ground black pepper
- ☐ ¹/₂ cup/125 g butter, melted and cooled
- ☐ 1 egg, lightly beaten
- ☐ ²/₃ cup/170 mL evaporated milk
- ☐ 1 cup/250 mL warm water
- ☐ whole wheat flour
- ☐ corn meal

1 Dissolve yeast in lukewarm water and set aside until mixture is frothy.
2 Combine flours with sugar, salt, herbs, onion flakes and black pepper to taste in a large mixing bowl. Combine butter, egg, milk and water. Make a well in the center of flour mixture and pour in butter and yeast mixtures and mix to form a soft dough.
3 Turn onto a lightly floured surface and knead for 5-8 minutes or until dough is smooth and elastic. Divide dough into six equal portions and roll each into a long sausage, tapering slightly at ends. Braid three portions together to form a loaf. Repeat with remaining dough.
4 Cover a cake rack with a clean cloth and lightly dust with whole wheat flour. Place loaves on rack, cover with plastic food wrap and stand in a warm, draught-free place for 30 minutes or until doubled in size.
5 Lift loaves carefully onto hot cookie sheets lightly dusted with corn meal and bake for 30-35 minutes, or until golden and base sounds hollow when tapped with fingers.
Variation: Divide dough in half, roll out one piece to a rectangle 8 x 12 in/ 20 x 30 cm. Roll up to make a long thin loaf. Make four or five slashes with a sharp knife across top of loaf. Repeat with remaining dough and cook as above.

WHOLE WHEAT COTTAGE LOAF

In Roman times white bread was reserved for the aristocracy, while rougher darker breads were for the poor.

Makes 1 loaf
Oven temperature 400°F/200°C

- ☐ 1 teaspoon brown sugar
- ☐ 1³/₄ cups/440 mL warm water
- ☐ 4 teaspoons dried yeast
- ☐ 2 cups/300 g whole wheat flour, sifted and chaff returned
- ☐ 2 cups/250 g flour, sifted
- ☐ 1 teaspoon salt
- ☐ 4 teaspoons sugar
- ☐ 1 tablespoon/15 g butter
- ☐ 1 egg, lightly beaten
- ☐ 4 teaspoons sesame seeds

1 Dissolve brown sugar in water, then sprinkle yeast over and set aside in a draught-free place for 10 minutes or until mixture is frothy.
2 Place flours, salt and sugar in a bowl and mix to combine. Rub in butter and make a well in the center and pour in yeast mixture. Mix to form a soft dough. Turn onto a lightly floured surface and knead for 5-8 minutes or until dough is smooth and elastic.
3 Place in a lightly greased bowl, cover with plastic food wrap and set aside to stand in a warm, draught-free place, for 30 minutes or until dough is doubled in size.
4 Punch down and turn onto a lightly floured surface and knead for 5 minutes or until smooth. Divide dough into two, making one portion twice the size of the other. Shape both portions of dough into round balls. Place the larger ball onto a lightly greased cookie sheet and flatten slightly. Using your index and second fingers make an indentation in the center of the ball. Dampen top of larger ball with a little water and place smaller ball on it. To secure, push your index and second fingers through the top to the base. Brush with egg and sprinkle with sesame seeds. Cover with plastic food wrap and set aside in a warm, draught-free place for 30 minutes or until dough is doubled in size.
5 Bake for 30-40 minutes or until the base sounds hollow when tapped with fingers.
Whole Wheat Rolls: Shape dough into a long sausage shape, then cut into even-sized pieces. Roll each piece of dough to form a small ball. Brush rolls with egg and sprinkle with sesame seeds. Place on greased oven trays, cover with plastic food wrap and set aside to rise. Bake for 20-25 minutes or until cooked. This quantity of dough will make 10 rolls.

HAZELNUT BREAD

Serves 8
Oven temperature 400°F/200°C

- ☐ 3 cups/375 g flour, sifted
- ☐ 1 cup/125 g rye flour, sifted
- ☐ 1 tablespoon dried yeast
- ☐ 2 teaspoons salt
- ☐ 2 eggs, lightly beaten
- ☐ 1 cup/250 mL warm water
- ☐ ³/₄ cup/125 g roughly chopped hazelnuts, toasted

EGG GLAZE
- ☐ 1 egg yolk, lightly beaten
- ☐ 1 tablespoon water
- ☐ pinch salt

1 Place flours, yeast and salt in a large mixing bowl. Stir in eggs and sufficient water to make a soft dough. Turn dough out onto a floured surface and knead for 5-8 minutes or until smooth and elastic. Place dough in a large, greased bowl, cover with plastic food wrap and set aside in a warm draught-free place until doubled in size.
2 Punch down and turn dough onto a lightly floured surface and knead in hazelnuts. Divide dough in half, shape each half into an oval shape and place on a greased cookie sheet. Cover loosely with plastic food wrap and set aside in a warm, draught-free place for 30 minutes or until doubled in size.
3 To make glaze, combine egg yolk, water and salt. Brush loaf with glaze and bake for 30-35 minutes or until golden. Remove from oven and cool on a wire rack.

Scones with Mixed-Berry Jam (page 35)

MILK BREAD

Makes 1 large loaf
Oven temperature 350°F/180°C

- [ ] **6 teaspoons sugar**
- [ ] **1¹/₃ cups/330 mL milk, warmed**
- [ ] **4 teaspoons dried yeast**
- [ ] **4 cups/500 g plain flour, sifted**
- [ ] **2 teaspoons salt**
- [ ] **2 tablespoons/30 g butter**
- [ ] **1 egg yolk, lightly beaten**
- [ ] **2 tablespoons sesame or poppy seeds**

1   Dissolve 2 teaspoons sugar in milk, then sprinkle over yeast and set aside in a warm, draught-free place for 10 minutes or until frothy.

2   Combine flour, salt and remaining sugar in a large mixing bowl. Rub in butter and make a well in the center, then pour in yeast mixture and egg yolk. Mix to form a soft dough. Turn onto a lightly floured surface and knead for 5-8 minutes, or until dough is smooth and elastic.

3   Place in a lightly greased bowl, cover with plastic food wrap and set aside to stand in a warm, draught-free place for 30 minutes, or until dough is doubled in size.

4   Punch down and turn onto a lightly floured surface and knead for 5 minutes or until smooth. Divide dough into two equal portions and roll each into a strip 4 in/10 cm wide and ¹/₂ in/1 cm thick. Roll up each strip from the short end and place rolls side by side in a large, greased and floured bread pan. Cover with plastic food wrap and set aside in a warm, draught-free place for 30 minutes or until doubled in size. Brush loaf with a little milk and sprinkle with sesame seeds.

5   Bake for 50-55 minutes, or until base sounds hollow when tapped with fingers.

'Tsuto'
Rural Japanese packaging

SCONES

The word 'scone' is believed to have come from the Gaelic word 'sgonn' – meaning large mouthful.

Makes 12
Oven temperature 425°F/220°C

- [ ] **2 cups/250 g self-rising flour**
- [ ] **1 teaspoon baking powder**
- [ ] **2 teaspoons sugar**
- [ ] **3 tablespoons/45 g butter**
- [ ] **1 egg**
- [ ] **¹/₂ cup/125 mL milk**

1   Sift together flour and baking powder into a large mixing bowl. Stir in sugar, then rub in butter using fingertips until mixture resembles coarse bread crumbs.

2   Whisk together egg and milk. Make a well in center of flour mixture and pour in egg mixture. Mix to form a soft dough, turn onto a floured surface and knead lightly.

3   Press dough out to a 1 in/2 cm thickness, using palm of hand. Cut out scones using a floured 2 in/5 cm cutter. Avoid twisting the cutter or the scones will rise unevenly.

4   Arrange close together on a greased and lightly floured cookie sheet or in an 8 in/20 cm shallow cake pan. Brush with a little milk and bake for 12-15 minutes or until golden brown.

SPICY COCONUT APPLE TWISTS

Makes 2 loaves
Oven temperature 350°F/180°C

- ☐ **2 cups/250 g flour, sifted**
- ☐ **¹/₂ teaspoon salt**
- ☐ **¹/₂ teaspoon ground cinnamon**
- ☐ **¹/₄ teaspoon ground cloves**
- ☐ **2-3 tablespoons sugar**
- ☐ **¹/₂ oz/15 g fresh yeast**
- ☐ **³/₄ cup/185 mL warm milk**
- ☐ **3 tablespoons/45 g butter, melted**
- ☐ **³/₄ cup/170 g canned apple slices**
- ☐ **¹/₄ teaspoon ground cinnamon**

COCONUT ICING
- ☐ **³/₄ cup/125 g confectioners' sugar, sifted**
- ☐ **1 tablespoon/15 g butter**
- ☐ **¹/₂ teaspoon vanilla extract**
- ☐ **¹/₃ cup shredded coconut**
- ☐ **4-5 tablespoons hot water**

1   Combine flour, salt, cinnamon, cloves and sugar in a mixing bowl. Dissolve yeast in milk and stand in a warm, draught-free place for 10 minutes or until mixture is frothy. Add to flour mixture with butter and mix to form a soft dough. Turn onto a lightly floured surface and knead for 5-8 minutes, or until dough is smooth and elastic. Place in a lightly greased bowl, cover with plastic food wrap and set aside to stand for 10 minutes.

2   Divide dough into four portions and roll each into a 3 x 12 in/8 x 30 cm strip. Spoon apple down center of each strip and sprinkle with cinnamon. Fold in half lengthwise and seal edges. Roll each into a sausage shape. Twist 2 rolls together and place on a greased cookie sheet. Repeat with remaining rolls.

3   Cover with plastic food wrap and allow to stand in a warm, draught-free place for 20 minutes or until doubled in size. Bake for 20-25 minutes, or until golden and cooked through.

4   To make icing, combine sugar, butter, vanilla extract, coconut and enough water to mix to a thin consistency. Spread icing over twists while they are still hot.

Divide dough into four portions and roll each into a 3 x 12 in/ 8 x 30 cm strip.

Spoon apple down center of each strip and sprinkle with cinnamon. Fold in half lengthwise and seal edges.

Roll each strip into a sausage shape. Twist 2 rolls together.

CHELSEA BUN

Mr Richard Hand, known as 'Captain Bun', ran the Chelsea Bun House in London in the late seventeenth century and it was there that the first Chelsea Bun was made. Captain Bun would be proud of this recipe for Chelsea Bun.

Serves 6
Oven temperature 350°F/180°C

- [ ] **1 quantity Scones recipe (page 41)**
- [ ] **¹/₄ cup/60 g butter**
- [ ] **¹/₃ cup/60g brown sugar**
- [ ] **1 teaspoon ground pumpkin pie spice**
- [ ] **8 oz/250 g mixed dried fruit**

SUGAR GLAZE
- [ ] **4 teaspoons water**
- [ ] **4 teaspoons sugar**
- [ ] **1 teaspoon gelatine**

1   Make up scone dough as directed. Roll out dough on a lightly floured surface to form an 8 x 12 in/20 x 30 cm rectangle.
2   Place butter, brown sugar and pumpkin pie spice in a bowl and beat until smooth. Spread over dough, then sprinkle with fruit. Roll up lengthwise and cut into eight thick slices using a sharp knife. Arrange slices in a greased, shallow 8 in/20 cm cake pan and bake for 25-30 minutes or until golden.
3   To make glaze, place water, sugar and gelatine in a saucepan and cook over a low heat, stirring constantly, until sugar and gelatine dissolve. Brush bun with glaze while hot. Serve warm or cold.

RAISIN PANCAKES

If you wish to make plain pancakes omit spice and raisins from this recipe.

Makes 20 pancakes

- [ ] **1 cup/125 g flour**
- [ ] **1 teaspoon baking powder**
- [ ] **1 teaspoon ground pumpkin pie spice**
- [ ] **¹/₄ cup/60 g superfine sugar**
- [ ] **¹/₄ cup/40 g chopped raisins**
- [ ] **1 egg, lightly beaten**
- [ ] **¹/₂ cup/125 mL milk**
- [ ] **¹/₃ cup/80 mL cream**

1   Sift together flour, baking powder and pumpkin pie spice into a large mixing bowl. Stir in sugar and raisins, then make a well in center of mixture.
2   Combine egg, milk and cream and gradually stir into dry ingredients until mixture is smooth.
3   Cook tablespoonfuls of mixture in a heated, greased, heavy-based skillet until bubbles appear on the surface, then turn and cook until golden brown.

BREADMAKER'S TIP

The protein content and age of the flour affect the absorption of the water and sometimes you will find that extra water may be required to achieve the right consistency for a bread dough.

Salt is an important ingredient in breadmaking. While it is not essential the lack of it is very noticeable. Too little salt tends to leave the bread tasting flat and the dough feeling slack during kneading. Too much salt, however, makes the bread taste bitter and will slow the yeast activity.

Chelsea Bun, Raisin Pancakes, Pecan Fruit Loaf

PECAN FRUIT LOAF

Serves 8
Oven temperature 350°F/180°C

- [ ] **2 cups/315 g mixed dried fruit**
- [ ] **1 cup/250 mL water**
- [ ] **1/2 cup/125 g butter**
- [ ] **1 1/2 cups/125 g sugar**
- [ ] **1 egg**
- [ ] **2 cups/250 g self-rising flour**
- [ ] **1/2 teaspoon baking powder**
- [ ] **1 cup/100 g pecans, roughly chopped**

1 Place fruit and water in a large saucepan, bring to a boil and cook for 3 minutes. Remove pan from heat and set aside to cool.
2 Place butter and sugar in a mixing bowl and beat until light and creamy. Add egg and continue to beat until well combined. Sift together flour and baking powder. Mix flour mixture and undrained fruit mixture alternately into butter mixture. Fold in pecans.
3 Spoon batter into a greased and lined 6 x 8 in/14 x 21 cm loaf pan and bake for 1 1/4 hours or until golden. Leave in pan for 5 minutes before turning onto a wire rack to cool.

breadmaking TECHNIQUES

Proofing: The process of activating yeast. Sprinkle or crumble yeast and a little sugar over warm liquid and stir gently. Set aside until yeast is frothy and creamy. The ideal water temperature for activating yeast is 102-108°F/ 40-46°C – a drop of liquid dropped on your wrist should feel comfortably warm. Yeast cells become dormant below 50°F/10°C and are killed at temperatures of 130°F/60°C.

Kneading: During kneading, the protein in flour, gluten, becomes elastic. To knead dough, lightly flour hands and work surface, then turn dough onto surface and gently bring far edge of dough forward and fold it over itself. Using the heel of your hand push dough away from you, then give it a quarter turn and repeat the process, until dough is smooth and elastic. Kneading by hand will take about 10 minutes. Flour should be used sparingly.

Rising: Place dough in a lightly greased large, deep glass or plastic bowl. Cover with plastic food wrap or a damp cloth. Place in a warm draught-free place until dough is doubled in size.

Baking: Place bread in center to lower third of oven. Baking kills the yeast and within the first 10 minutes the rapidly expanding gases will have reached their limit, then the heat will set the gluten cells. Bread is baked at temperatures between 350°F/ 180°C and 425°F/220°C. Breads without fat, such as French bread, are baked at higher temperatures, while richer more cakelike doughs using butter, fruit and nuts are baked at lower temperatures.

a day in the
COUNTRY

The picnic hamper

*F*resh air, blue sky and good food are a great combination. Be adventurous with your picnic fare – the days of cold chicken, lettuce and tomatoes are long gone!

From left: Lemonade, Pear and Hazelnut Tart, Vegetable Frittata, Roast Pepper Salad, French Country Terrine, Herbed Mountain Trout

ROAST PEPPER SALAD

A colorful, strongly flavored salad of Mediterranean origin. If yellow peppers are unavailable, use three green and three red peppers instead. To allow the flavors to develop fully make the salad 2-3 hours before serving.

Serves 6
Oven temperature 400°F/200°C

- [ ] **2 red peppers, quartered**
- [ ] **2 green peppers, quartered**
- [ ] **2 yellow peppers, quartered**
- [ ] **freshly ground black pepper**

BASIL DRESSING
- [ ] **12 fresh basil leaves, chopped**
- [ ] **1 clove garlic, crushed**
- [ ] **1/2 cup/125 mL olive oil**
- [ ] **1/4 cup/60 mL red wine vinegar**

1   Place red, green and yellow peppers under a preheated grill and cook until skins blister and char. Place in a paper or freezer bag and set aside for 10 minutes or until cool enough to handle. Remove skins from peppers, cut into strips and place in a bowl.
2   To make dressing, combine basil, garlic, oil and vinegar in a small jar and shake well to combine. Spoon over peppers and toss to combine. Season to taste with black pepper, cover and refrigerate until required.

HERBED MOUNTAIN TROUT

Serves 4

- [ ] **2 trout, cleaned**
- [ ] **3 tablespoons lime juice**
- [ ] **1 lime, sliced**
- [ ] **1 lemon, sliced**
- [ ] **freshly ground black pepper**
- [ ] **1/4 cup/60 mL olive oil**
- [ ] **1 large bunch mixed fresh herbs, such as rosemary, sage and parsley**

1   Wipe cavities of trout, then brush with lime juice and fill with lime and lemon slices. Season to taste with black pepper.
2   Brush trout with oil and tie herbs around them with string. Place trout on a heated grill and cook for 10-15 minutes each side, or until fish flakes when tested.

LEMONADE

A refreshing drink for a hot day.

Serves 10

- [ ] **5 large lemons**
- [ ] **1 1/2 cups/375 g sugar**
- [ ] **3/4 cup/185 mL water**

1   Grate rind of 1 lemon and set aside. Squeeze all lemons, strain juice and set aside.
2   Place sugar, water and lemon rind in a saucepan and cook over a medium heat, stirring constantly, until sugar dissolves. Bring to a boil and cook for 3 minutes. Remove from heat and set aside to cool.
3   Stir lemon juice into sugar syrup and pour into a clean bottle.
To serve: Use one part lemon syrup to two parts water or soda water.

VEGETABLE FRITTATA

Serves 6

- [ ] **2-3 tablespoons olive oil**
- [ ] **1 onion, finely sliced**
- [ ] **2 stalks celery, sliced**
- [ ] **1 leek, finely sliced**
- [ ] **1 large red pepper, cut into strips**
- [ ] **2 zucchini, sliced**
- [ ] **8 oz/250 g button mushrooms, sliced**
- [ ] **6 eggs**
- [ ] **1/4 cup/60 mL cream**
- [ ] **freshly ground black pepper**
- [ ] **1 cup/315 g canned corn kernels, drained**
- [ ] **4 slices whole wheat bread, crusts removed and cut into cubes**
- [ ] **3 tablespoons grated Parmesan cheese**
- [ ] **4 teaspoons finely chopped fresh parsley**
- [ ] **4 teaspoons finely chopped fresh dill**
- [ ] **12 spears fresh asparagus, blanched**
- [ ] **1 cup/125 g grated sharp cheese**

1   Heat oil in a large skillet and cook onion, celery, leek and red pepper for 4-5 minutes. Add zucchini and mushrooms and cook for 10 minutes longer. Remove pan from heat and set aside to cool for 10 minutes.
2   Whisk together eggs and cream, and season to taste with black pepper. Mix in corn, bread cubes, Parmesan cheese, parsley and dill. Add cooked vegetables and mix to combine.
3   Pour mixture into a greased 10 in/25 cm skillet. Arrange asparagus spears like spokes of a wheel on top of frittata and sprinkle with sharp cheese. Cook over a low heat for 15 minutes or until firm. Place under a preheated broiler and cook for 3-4 minutes or until top is lightly browned.

FRENCH COUNTRY TERRINE

Serves 8
Oven temperature 350°F/180°C

- [ ] 2 lb/1 kg lean ground pork and veal
- [ ] 6¹/₂ oz/200 g leg ham, chopped
- [ ] 1 large onion, chopped
- [ ] 2 cloves garlic, crushed
- [ ] 2 cups/125 g bread crumbs, made from stale bread
- [ ] ¹/₄ cup/60 mL dry sherry
- [ ] 2 tablespoons Dijon mustard
- [ ] 3 eggs, lightly beaten
- [ ] 2 teaspoons dried rosemary
- [ ] 1 teaspoon ground sage
- [ ] freshly ground black pepper
- [ ] 4 slices bacon, trimmed
- [ ] ¹/₂ tablespoon gelatine
- [ ] 1 cup/250 mL hot chicken stock
- [ ] fresh tarragon sprigs

1 Place meat, onion, garlic, bread crumbs, sherry, mustard, eggs, rosemary and sage in a large bowl. Mix well to combine. Season to taste with black pepper.
2 Spoon mixture into a large greased ovenproof terrine or loaf dish. Cover top with bacon and place in a baking dish with enough water to come halfway up the sides of terrine. Cover and bake for 1¹/₂ hours or until firm and cooked through. Remove from oven, drain off any juices, then weigh down and set aside to cool completely.
3 Combine gelatine and hot chicken stock and set aside until mixture begins to thicken and set. Turn terrine onto a board and arrange tarragon sprigs over bacon, then spoon over gelatine mixture and set aside until firm. Cut into slices to serve.

Cook's tip: If ground veal is unavailable you can use ground chicken in its place. This will give a terrine with a different flavor but it is just as delicious.

PEAR AND HAZELNUT TART

Serves 8
Oven temperature 350°F/180°C

PASTRY
- [ ] 1¹/₄ cups/155 g flour, sifted
- [ ] ¹/₄ cup/60 g superfine sugar
- [ ] 6 tablespoons/90 g butter
- [ ] 2 egg yolks, lightly beaten
- [ ] 4 teaspoons iced water

PEAR AND HAZELNUT FILLING
- [ ] ¹/₂ cup/125 g butter, softened
- [ ] ¹/₃ cup/75 g sugar
- [ ] 2 eggs
- [ ] 1 cup/100 g hazelnuts, ground
- [ ] 1 tablespoon flour
- [ ] 4 small pears, cored, peeled and halved

APRICOT GLAZE
- [ ] 2 tablespoons apricot jam
- [ ] 1 tablespoon brandy

1 To make pastry, place flour and sugar in a large mixing bowl. Rub in butter using fingertips until mixture resembles coarse bread crumbs. Mix in egg yolks and enough water to form a firm dough. Turn dough onto a floured surface and knead lightly. Cover and refrigerate for 30 minutes.
2 To make filling, place butter and sugar in a large mixing bowl and beat until just combined. Add eggs one at a time, beating well after each addition. Fold in hazelnuts and flour.
3 Roll out pastry and place in greased 9 in/23 cm tart pan with a removable base. Spread hazelnut mixture over pastry. Arrange pear halves over filling and bake for 45-50 minutes or until golden. Remove from oven and set aside to cool slightly.
4 To make glaze, combine apricot jam and brandy in a saucepan and cook over a low heat, stirring constantly, until jam melts. Strain and brush top of tart with glaze.

COUNTRY BARBECUE

Nothing beats the flavor of freshly caught trout. Be optimistic and take your trout fishing and cooking equipment – but just in case the fish don't bite make sure you have a back-up lunch in your picnic basket. Pack a small barbecue to cook your trout and don't forget the firestarters. Remember to take the ingredients to add that special touch to your trout.

picnic CHECKLIST

A picnic is more pleasurable if you have everything to make it the perfect day. Laying out your picnic and finding that you have no knives and forks can make eating a problem! Use this checklist to ensure that you have packed everything you will need.

- [ ] knives and forks
- [ ] plates (unbreakable are best)
- [ ] glasses (unbreakable are best)
- [ ] napkins (paper or cloth)
- [ ] mugs
- [ ] chopping board
- [ ] serrated knife for cutting bread
- [ ] knives suitable for cutting meats, pies, fruit and vegetables
- [ ] corkscrew and bottle opener
- [ ] salt and pepper
- [ ] damp cloth for wiping sticky fingers
- [ ] cool drink
- [ ] tea or coffee
- [ ] thermos of hot water
- [ ] milk
- [ ] sugar
- [ ] butter, if you are planning to serve bread or rolls at the picnic
- [ ] trash bags (so that you can take away your trash)
- [ ] sun hats
- [ ] sunscreen
- [ ] insect repellent
- [ ] first aid kit

If you are having a barbecue remember also to include:
- [ ] grill
- [ ] barbecue tools
- [ ] firestarters
- [ ] matches
- [ ] wood or coals (if you are unsure of the supply at your picnic site)

THE PERFECT PICNIC SET

Complement your delicious picnic with a set of coordinated picnic practicalities. Make the plastic-backed cloth, napkins, plate pouch, cutlery bag and bottle cover in a crisp, country polycotton

MATERIALS
- ☐ 2¹/₂ yds/2.5 m of 45 in/115 cm wide or wider fabric
- ☐ 2¹/₂ yds/2.5 m of 36 in/90 cm wide or wider plastic
- ☐ matching sewing thread
- ☐ 1 yd/1 m felt-back protective table covering or felt
- ☐ 3¹/₄ yds/3 m of 1 in/2.5 cm wide ribbon
- ☐ 2¹/₄ yds/2 m of narrow piping
- ☐ 2 yds/1.75 m of ³/₄ in/2 cm wide lace edging
- ☐ 20 yds/17 m of 1¹/₂ in/3.5 cm wide lace edging
- ☐ ¹/₂ yd/0.5 m of 36 in/90 cm wide felt for plate pouch or use protective table covering
- ☐ ¹/₂ yd/0.5 m of ³/₈ in/1 cm wide ribbon

TABLECLOTH
Makes a 45 in/115 cm square tablecloth
1 Cut one 45 in/115 cm square of fabric and one of plastic. If necessary join pieces to give correct size.
2 Pin the plastic to the wrong side of the fabric. Stitch together using a ¹/₂ in/0.5 m seam. From here on treat as one piece.
3 Cut 5³/₄ yds/5.2 m of 1¹/₂ in lace edging. This length will allow for mitering corners. Press ¹/₂ in/0.5 cm on the raw edge of the lace to the wrong side.
4 Matching the decorative edge and the raw edge of the cloth, place the lace on the right side of the fabric and pin in place, making sure to miter each corner and match lace edging as you go. Using a small zigzag stitch, attach lace to cloth, stitching evenly and neatly along the fold of lace. Trim off excess fabric beneath the lace edging.

NAPKINS
Makes 4 napkins
1 Cut four 13 in/35 cm squares of fabric.
2 Divide the ³/₄ in/2 cm wide lace edging into four equal lengths.
3 Sew napkins using the same method as the tablecloth, but eliminating the plastic liner.

Made of a crisp polycotton, this picnic set has a plastic-backed cloth, napkins, plate pouch, cutlery bag and bottle cover that are sure to complement any feast

PLATE POUCH

1   Cut one 13 in/35 cm square of fabric and one of protective table covering. Place the covering on the wrong side of the fabric and stitch around the edge to secure. From here on treat as one piece.

2   Cut two rectangles of fabric, each 7 x 13 in/19 x 35 cm. Place piping on the right side of the fabric along one long edge. Stitch close to the piping.

3   Cut two rectangles of protective table covering, each 7 x 13 in/19 x 35 cm. Place the right side of the protective covering against the right side of the fabric with the piping in between. Stitch through all thicknesses along the previous stitchline. Fold protective covering to the wrong side and press. Repeat for the other half.

4   With right sides together, pin both top sections on base section. Piped center edges meet at the center. Stitch around the edge, using a $\frac{1}{2}$ in/1 cm seam.

5   Turn the pouch right side out and press gently.

6   Cut $\frac{3}{8}$ in/1 cm wide ribbon into two equal lengths. Stitch ends on either side of center piping. Tie in a bow.

TOOL AND CUTLERY BAG

Lined with plastic, this useful bag can easily be wiped clean when soiled.

1   Cut a rectangle of fabric and one of plastic for lining, 24 x 10 in/60 x 25 cm. With right sides facing, fold the fabric into a 12 x 10 in/30 x 25 cm rectangle. Stitch side seam using $\frac{1}{2}$ in/ 1 cm seams. To miter the base corners, fold the seam at right angles to the base. Stitch across

through all thicknesses, 1 in/3 cm from the point. Repeat for the other corner.

2   Repeat Step 1 for the plastic lining.
Note: Do not backstitch on plastic. Leave long thread ends at the beginning of seams and gently pull these to 'ease' the plastic under presser foot.

3   Turn the fabric bag right side out. Slide the plastic lining inside the fabric bag, matching side seams. Edgestitch around the top of the bag, joining lining and fabric. From here on treat as a single layer.

4   Measure around the top of the bag. Cut the wide lace to this measurement plus $\frac{3}{4}$ in/2 cm. Join the lace ends using a French seam. (See How to Sew French Seams.) Attach the lace to the bag top using a French seam.

5   Stitch the center of a 29 in/75 cm strip of 1 in/2.5 cm wide ribbon to one side of the bag, 2 in/5 cm below the lace edging. Tie in a bow.

BOTTLE COVER

1   Cut two strips of fabric each 25 x 4 in/ 65 x 10 cm. Find the center of each strip. Place strips so that they cross at the center with right sides down. Pin where the fabrics cross – this will be the base. Using a small satin stitch, join along the raw edges on the right side.

2   With right sides facing, join the side seams from base to top using a $\frac{1}{4}$ in/ 5 mm seam. Overlock or neatly finish seam edges with a fine zigzag stitch. Turn right side out.

3   Attach lace and ribbon in the same way as for the Tool Bag.

4   For the lining, cut two strips of protective covering, each 23 x 8$\frac{1}{2}$ in/60 x 9 cm. Sew in the same way as for the cover, omitting French seams. Trim seam allowances to $\frac{1}{8}$ in/3 mm. Slide the lining inside the cover with wrong sides facing.

HINTS AND TIPS

❧ Handwash items and dry them flat, out of the sun.

❧ Use a plastic shower curtain in place of the plastic. This will eliminate joining pieces, be more economical and one curtain will be sufficient for the whole set.

❧ Use fabrics with some polyester content to prevent heavy creasing as ironing is difficult with the plastic lining. Adjust the measurements to suit your basket.

❧ If you need to join plastic for the Tablecloth, overlap the seam edges and stitch with a medium straight stitch. A roller foot can make sewing on plastic easier, but is not absolutely necessary.

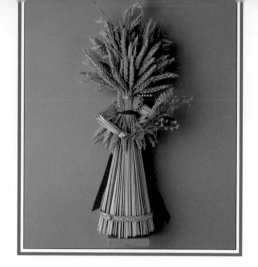

the pastry CRUST

Pies and tarts

*U*ntil the eighteenth century, pies contained a mixture of sweet and savory ingredients in a crust that was merely a container to hold the filling. This delicious selection will introduce you to the art of piemaking. Try making Individual Meat Pies, an Old English Pork Pie or a high-rise Lemon and Lime Meringue Pie.

Top: Wheat weaving 'Harvest Maid'
Right: Bacon, Leek and Apple Pie, Individual Meat Pies, High-Rise Apple Pie (all recipes page 54)

HIGH-RISE APPLE PIE

For an exotic change, spice your apple pie with ground cardamom rather than cinnamon.

Serves 8
Oven temperature 425°F/220°C

PASTRY
- ☐ **3 cups/375 g flour, sifted**
- ☐ **4 teaspoons confectioners' sugar, sifted**
- ☐ **12 tablespoons/185 g butter, chilled**
- ☐ **$^1/_2$ cup/125 mL iced water**
- ☐ **1 egg white, lightly beaten**
- ☐ **sugar**

APPLE FILLING
- ☐ **6 large cooking apples, cored, peeled and sliced**
- ☐ **$^1/_2$ teaspoon ground cinnamon**
- ☐ **2 tablespoons flour**
- ☐ **$^1/_3$ cup/90 g sugar**
- ☐ **2 tablespoon/30 g butter, cut into small pieces**

1 To make pastry, combine flour and confectioners' sugar in a large mixing bowl. Rub in butter using fingertips until mixture resembles coarse bread crumbs. Mix in enough water to form a firm dough. Turn pastry onto a floured surface and knead lightly until smooth. Cover and refrigerate for 30 minutes.
2 Roll out three-quarters of the pastry on a lightly floured surface and place in a lightly greased, deep 8 in/20 cm pie dish. Trim edges with a sharp knife.
3 To make filling, place apple slices, cinnamon, flour and sugar in a bowl and mix to combine. Arrange apples in pastry shell, shaping apples to a dome in the center. Dot with butter.
4 Roll out remaining pastry on a lightly floured surface until large enough to cover pie. Brush edge of shell with water and cover with top. Press edges together to seal, then trim and make a decorative edge using fingertips. Make two slits in top of pie to allow steam to escape. Brush with egg white, sprinkle with sugar and bake for 20 minutes. Reduce temperature to 350°F/ 180°C and cook for 40-45 minutes longer, or until apples are tender when tested with a skewer.

BACON, LEEK AND APPLE PIE

A wonderful combination of flavors, this pie is delicious hot, warm or cold.

Serves 8
Oven temperature 425°F/220°C

PASTRY
- ☐ **2 cups/250 g flour, sifted**
- ☐ **$^1/_2$ cup/125 g butter**
- ☐ **5-6 tablespoons iced water**

APPLE AND LEEK FILLING
- ☐ **1 tablespoon/15 g butter**
- ☐ **1 cooking apple, cored, peeled and sliced**
- ☐ **3 small leeks, washed, trimmed and sliced**
- ☐ **4 slices bacon, trimmed and chopped**
- ☐ **$^1/_4$ teaspoon ground cloves**
- ☐ **$^1/_4$ teaspoon ground nutmeg**
- ☐ **2 oz/60 g blue cheese, crumbled**
- ☐ **3 eggs, lightly beaten**
- ☐ **$^3/_4$ cup/185 mL cream**
- ☐ **3 tablespoons port**
- ☐ **freshly ground black pepper**

1 To make pastry, place flour in a large mixing bowl, rub in butter with fingertips until mixture resembles coarse bread crumbs. Mix in enough water to form a firm dough. Turn pastry onto a floured surface and knead lightly. Cover and refrigerate for 30 minutes.
2 To make filling, melt butter in a skillet and cook apple, leeks and bacon over a medium heat for 6-8 minutes or until apple softens. Add cloves and nutmeg to pan and cook for 1 minute. Remove pan from heat and set aside to cool.
3 Roll out pastry on a lightly floured surface and place in a greased 9 in/23 cm tart pan. Prick base and sides of pastry with a fork and bake for 10 minutes.
4 Spread apple mixture over base of pastry shell. Combine blue cheese, eggs, cream, port and black pepper to taste. Carefully pour mixture into pastry shell. Reduce temperature to 350°F/180°C and bake for 30-35 minutes or until set.

INDIVIDUAL MEAT PIES

An individual homemade pie served with mashed potatoes and peas was once the traditional working man's lunch and is still a great favorite. The secret to a really good pie is a generous filling with plenty of flavor.

Makes 8 individual pies
Oven temperature 425°F/220°C

- ☐ **24 oz/750 g prepared or ready-rolled pie crust pastry, thawed**
- ☐ **12 oz/375 g prepared or ready-rolled puff pastry, thawed**
- ☐ **1 egg, lightly beaten**

BEEF FILLING
- ☐ **$1^1/_2$ lb/750 g ground chuck**
- ☐ **2 cups/500 mL beef stock**
- ☐ **freshly ground black pepper**
- ☐ **$2^2/_3$ tablespoons corn starch blended with $^1/_2$ cup/125 mL water**
- ☐ **4 teaspoons Worcestershire sauce**
- ☐ **1 teaspoon soy sauce**

1 To make filling, heat a nonstick skillet and cook meat over a medium heat, stirring constantly, for 6-8 minutes or until meat browns. Drain pan of any juices and add stock. Season to taste with black pepper.
2 Bring mixture to a boil, then reduce heat, cover and simmer, stirring occasionally, for 20 minutes. Stir in corn starch mixture, Worcestershire and soy sauces and cook, stirring constantly, until mixture boils and thickens. Set aside to cool.
3 Line eight greased small metal pie pans with pie crust pastry. Cut rounds of puff pastry to fit top of pies. Divide filling between pie dishes. Brush edges of pie crust with water and top with rounds of puff pastry. Press edges together to seal. Brush with egg and bake for 5 minutes, then reduce temperature to 350°F/180°C and bake for 10-15 minutes or until top of pie is golden and crisp.

LEMON AND LIME MERINGUE PIE

This high-rise pie is sure to impress. The addition of lime gives it a wonderful tang. If limes are unavailable, replace them with additional lemons.

Serves 8
Oven temperature 400°F/200°C

PASTRY
- [ ] **12 tablespoons/185 g butter**
- [ ] **1/3 cup/75 g superfine sugar**
- [ ] **1 1/2 cups/185 g flour**
- [ ] **2/3 cup/90 g corn starch**

LEMON AND LIME FILLING
- [ ] **1/3 cup/45 g flour, sifted**
- [ ] **1/3 cup/36 g corn starch, sifted**
- [ ] **1 teaspoon finely grated lemon rind**
- [ ] **1 teaspoon finely grated lime rind**
- [ ] **1/2 cup/125 mL lemon juice**
- [ ] **1/4 cup/60 mL lime juice**
- [ ] **1 cup/250 g sugar**
- [ ] **1 1/4 cups/310 mL water**
- [ ] **6 tablespoons/90 g butter, chopped**
- [ ] **4 egg yolks, lightly beaten**

MERINGUE TOPPING
- [ ] **4 egg whites**
- [ ] **2 tablespoons water**
- [ ] **3/4 cup/170 g superfine sugar**

1   To make pastry, place butter and superfine sugar in a large mixing bowl and beat until light and creamy. Sift together flour and corn starch and gradually mix into butter mixture. Turn pastry onto a floured surface and knead lightly. Press mixture over base and sides of a greased, deep 9 in/23 cm pie dish. Prick base and sides with a fork and bake for 20-25 minutes or until golden. Remove from oven and set aside to cool.

2   To make filling, place flour, corn starch,

Lemon and Lime Meringue Pie

lemon rind, lime rind, lemon juice, lime juice, sugar and water in a saucepan and blend until smooth. Cook over a medium heat, stirring constantly, for 3-4 minutes or until mixture boils and thickens. Reduce heat and cook, stirring constantly, for 3 minutes longer.

3   Remove pan from heat and add butter and egg yolks. Stir until butter melts, then set aside to cool completely. Spread filling evenly over pastry shell and set aside.

4   To make topping, place egg whites and water in a large mixing bowl and beat until soft peaks form. Add sugar a little at a time, beating well after each addition. Continue to beat until mixture is glossy and stiff peaks form.

5   Spoon topping over filling, spreading to edge to seal. Bake at 350°F/180°C for 5-10 minutes or until lightly browned. Remove from oven and set aside to cool.

CORNISH PASTIES

Originally the portable lunch of the Cornish working man, these pasties are great eaten hot, warm or cold and are ideal for a picnic or lunch box.

Makes 6
Oven temperature 425°F/220°C

PASTRY
- ☐ ¹/₄ cup/60 g butter, softened
- ☐ 2 oz/60 g lard, softened
- ☐ 2 cups/250 g flour, sifted
- ☐ 5-6 tablespoons cold water
- ☐ 1 egg, lightly beaten

FILLING
- ☐ ¹/₂ lb/250 g ground chuck
- ☐ 1 small onion, grated
- ☐ 1 potato, peeled and grated
- ☐ ¹/₂ small turnip, peeled and grated
- ☐ 3 tablespoons finely chopped fresh parsley
- ☐ 4 teaspoons Worcestershire sauce
- ☐ freshly ground black pepper

From left: Cornish Pasties, Potato, Egg and Leek Pies, Old English Pork Pie

1 To make pastry, place butter and lard in a bowl and mix well to combine. Refrigerate until firm. Place flour in a large mixing bowl. Chop butter mixture into small pieces and rub in flour using fingertips until mixture resembles coarse bread crumbs. Mix in enough water to form a soft dough. Turn pastry onto a floured surface and knead lightly. Cover and refrigerate for 30 minutes.

2 To make filling, place meat, onion, potato, turnip, parsley, Worcestershire sauce and black pepper to taste in a bowl and mix well to combine.

3 Roll out pastry on a lightly floured surface and using an inverted saucer as a guide cut out six 6 in/15 cm rounds. Divide filling between pastry rounds. Brush edges with water and fold the pastry rounds in half upwards to enclose filling.

4 Press edges together well to seal, then flute between finger and thumb. Place pasties on a well greased oven tray. Brush with egg and bake for 15 minutes. Reduce temperature to 325°F/160°C and bake for 20 minutes or until golden.

POTATO, EGG AND LEEK PIES

Makes 8 individual pies
Oven temperature 425°F/220°C

- ☐ 2 lb/1 kg prepared or ready-rolled puff pastry
- ☐ 1 egg, lightly beaten

POTATO AND LEEK FILLING
- ☐ 2 tablespoons/30 g butter
- ☐ 4 leeks, sliced
- ☐ 2 cloves garlic, crushed
- ☐ 2 teaspoons curry powder
- ☐ 6 potatoes, peeled and cooked until tender
- ☐ 4 hard-boiled eggs, chopped
- ☐ 2 x 11 oz/350 g canned asparagus spears, drained
- ☐ 4 tablespoons chopped fresh parsley
- ☐ ²/₃ cup/170 g sour cream
- ☐ 1 cup (125 g) grated sharp cheese
- ☐ 2 egg yolks, lightly beaten
- ☐ freshly ground black pepper
- ☐ 1 egg, lightly beaten
- ☐ caraway seeds

1 To make filling, melt butter in a skillet and cook leeks over a low heat for 3-4 minutes or until soft. Stir in garlic and curry powder and cook over a medium heat for 1 minute. Remove pan from heat.

2 Chop potatoes and place in a bowl with leek mixture, chopped eggs, asparagus, parsley, sour cream, cheese and egg yolks. Season to taste with black pepper. Set aside to cool.

3 Using two-thirds of the pastry, line eight greased metal pie pans. Cut remaining pastry to fit top of pies. Spoon filling into pie shells and brush pastry edges with egg

and top with pie lids. Press edges together to seal. Make a slit on the top of each pie using a sharp knife. Brush tops of pies with egg and bake for 15 minutes. Reduce heat to 350°F/180°C and bake for 15 minutes or until golden brown.

OLD ENGLISH PORK PIE

Probably the most famous English pie, the pork pie dates back to the fourteenth century when it included raisins and currants. This pie is sure to be popular and is delicious as a picnic food.

Serves 8
Oven temperature 500°F/250°C

PASTRY
- ☐ **3 cups/375 g flour, sifted**
- ☐ **1 teaspoon salt**
- ☐ **4 oz/125 g lard**
- ☐ **1 cup/250 mL water**
- ☐ **1 egg yolk, lightly beaten with 1 tablespoon water**

FILLING
- ☐ **3 lb/1.5 kg lean boneless pork, cut into 1/4 in/5 mm cubes**
- ☐ **1/2 teaspoon ground sage**
- ☐ **freshly ground black pepper**
- ☐ **2 cups/500 mL chicken consommé**

1   To make pastry, place flour and salt in a large mixing bowl and make a well in the center.

2   Place lard and water in a saucepan and cook over a medium heat until lard melts and mixture boils. Pour boiling liquid into flour and mix to form a firm dough. Turn pastry onto a floured surface and knead lightly until smooth. Cover and set aside for 10 minutes.

3   Lightly knead two-thirds of pastry and roll out. Line base and sides of a greased deep 8 in/20 cm springform pan with pastry and bake for 15 minutes. Remove from oven and set aside to cool.

4   To make filling, combine pork, sage and black pepper to taste. Pack mixture firmly into pastry shell and brush edges with a little of the egg yolk mixture.

5   Knead remaining pastry, then roll out to a circle large enough to cover pie. Place pastry over filling, trim pastry and press top to pastry shell. Cut a 1 in/2.5 cm circle from center of pastry. Brush pastry with remaining egg yolk mixture and bake for 30 minutes. Reduce temperature to 325°F/160°C and bake for 1 1/2 hours. Using a spoon, remove any juices that appear in the hole during cooking. Remove from oven and set aside to cool in pan for 2 hours. Place chicken consommé in a saucepan and cook over a low heat until melted. Set aside to cool slightly, then gradually pour into pie through hole in the top. Allow to cool. Refrigerate pie overnight.

Tiles
Country Floors

BEEF AND MUSHROOM PIE

Serves 4
Oven temperature 425°F/220°C

PUFF PASTRY
- ☐ **6 tablespoons/90 g butter, softened**
- ☐ **3 oz/90 g lard, softened**
- ☐ **2 cups/250 g flour**
- ☐ **$^1/_2$ cup/125 mL cold water**

BEEF AND MUSHROOM FILLING
- ☐ **2 lb/1 kg lean chuck (beef), cut into 1 in/2.5 cm cubes**
- ☐ **$^1/_2$ cup/60 g flour**
- ☐ **$^1/_4$ cup/60 g butter**
- ☐ **$^1/_4$ cup/60 mL olive oil**
- ☐ **2 onions, chopped**
- ☐ **2 cloves garlic, crushed**
- ☐ **8 oz/250 g button mushrooms, sliced**
- ☐ **$^1/_2$ cup/125 mL red wine**
- ☐ **$^1/_2$ cup/125 mL beef stock**
- ☐ **1 bay leaf**
- ☐ **3 tablespoons finely chopped fresh parsley**
- ☐ **4 teaspoons Worcestershire sauce**
- ☐ **salt and freshly ground black pepper**
- ☐ **1 tablespoon corn starch blended with 2 tablespoons water**
- ☐ **1 egg, lightly beaten**

1   To make filling, toss meat in flour to coat. Shake off excess flour. Melt butter and oil in a large heavy-based saucepan and cook meat in batches for 3-4 minutes or until browned on all sides. Remove meat from pan and set aside.

2   Add onions and garlic to pan and cook over a medium heat for 3-4 minutes or until onion softens. Stir in mushrooms and cook for 2 minutes longer. Combine wine and stock, pour into pan and cook for 4-5 minutes, stirring constantly to lift sediment from base of pan. Bring to a boil, then reduce heat. Return meat to pan with bay leaf, parsley, Worcestershire sauce and black pepper to taste. Cover and simmer for 1$^1/_2$ hours or until meat is tender. Stir in corn starch mixture and cook, stirring, until mixture thickens. Remove pan from heat and set aside to cool.

3   To make pastry, place butter and lard in a bowl and mix until well combined. Cover and refrigerate until firm. Place flour in a large mixing bowl. Cut one-quarter of butter mixture into small pieces and rub into flour using fingertips until mixture resembles coarse bread crumbs. Mix in enough water to form a firm dough.

4   Turn pastry onto a floured surface and knead lightly. Roll pastry out to a 6 x 10 in/ 15 x 25 cm rectangle. Cut another one-quarter of butter mixture into small pieces and place over top two-thirds of pastry. Fold the bottom third of pastry up and top third of pastry down to give three even layers. Rotate pastry to have open end facing you and roll out to a rectangle as before. Repeat folding and rolling twice. Cover pastry and refrigerate for 1 hour.

5   Place cooled filling in a 4 cup (1 liter) oval pie dish. On a lightly floured surface, roll out pastry 2 in/4 cm larger than pie dish. Cut off a $^1/_2$ in/1 cm strip from pastry edge. Brush rim of dish with water and press pastry strip onto rim. Brush pastry strip with water. Lift pastry top over filling and press gently to seal edges. Trim and knock back edges to make a decorative edge. Brush with egg and bake for 30 minutes or until pastry is golden and crisp.

Cut one-quarter of butter mixture into small pieces and place over top two-thirds of pastry.

Fold the bottom third of pastry up and the top third of pastry down to give three even layers.

perfect PIES

Savory pies and tarts make substantial family dishes while sweet pies are among the most delicious desserts. Making your own pastry is easy and satisfying.

❧ When making pastry have all the utensils and ingredients as cold as possible. In hot weather chill the utensils before using. Wash your hands in cold water and use only your fingertips for kneading.

❧ Always add water or liquid cautiously as the amount required can vary depending on the flour used.

❧ A food processor is great for making pastry as the ingredients can be mixed together in seconds. When a recipe says to rub the fat in using fingertips, you can do this in the food processor using the metal blade, then add water to form a dough.

❧ When filling pies, fill the dish or pastry case to the rim. If the pie is to be covered, pile the filling in the center to help support the lid. If you do not have enough filling for the pie, place an inverted egg cup or a pie funnel in the middle of the dish for support.

❧ If the filling is cooked before it is put in the pie, the filling should be cold, or the pastry will be tough and soggy.

❧ Always preheat the oven before baking pastry. If pastry is put into a cold oven the fat will run and the pastry will be tough, greasy and have a poor texture.

❧ Uncooked pastry can be stored in an airtight container or sealed plastic food bag in the refrigerator for up to 3 days, or frozen for up to 3 months. Before freezing pastry, roll and shape it.

PEAR AND FIG TART

Serves 8
Oven temperature 425°F/220°C

HAZELNUT PASTRY
- ☐ **2 cups/250 g flour, sifted**
- ☐ **$^1/_4$ cup/45 g finely chopped hazelnuts**
- ☐ **1 teaspoon pumpkin pie spice**
- ☐ **$^3/_4$ cup/185 g butter, chilled and cut into small cubes**
- ☐ **1 egg yolk, lightly beaten with a few drops vanilla extract**
- ☐ **4-6 tablespoons water, chilled**

PEAR AND FIG FILLING
- ☐ **6 tablespoons/90 g butter**
- ☐ **4 pears, peeled, cored and quartered**
- ☐ **$3^1/_2$ oz/100 g dried figs, chopped**
- ☐ **$^1/_2$ cup/125 g brown sugar**
- ☐ **$^1/_2$ cup/125 mL light molasses**
- ☐ **$^1/_2$ cup/125 mL water**
- ☐ **$^1/_2$ teaspoon vanilla extract**
- ☐ **$^1/_2$ cup/60 g flour**
- ☐ **1 egg, lightly beaten**

1 To make pastry, place flour, hazelnuts and pumpkin pie spice in a mixing bowl and rub in butter using fingertips until the mixture resembles fine bread crumbs. Mix in egg yolk mixture and enough water, using a flexible metal spatula, to form a soft dough. Turn dough onto a lightly floured surface and knead gently until smooth. Wrap dough in plastic food wrap and refrigerate for 30 minutes.

2 Roll out pastry on a lightly floured surface. Line a lightly greased deep 9 in/ 23 cm tart pan and refrigerate for 15 minutes. Line pastry with wax paper and uncooked rice and bake blind for 10 minutes then remove rice and paper and bake for 10 minutes longer.

3 To make filling, cut each pear quarter into four slices. Melt half the butter in a skillet and cook pears for 4-5 minutes. Remove pears from pan and arrange over pastry shell, then sprinkle with figs.

4 Place sugar, molasses, water, remaining butter and vanilla extract in a saucepan and cook over a medium heat until sugar dissolves. Bring to a boil and simmer for 2 minutes.

5 Remove from heat and set aside to cool for 15 minutes, then beat in flour and egg. Pour over pears and figs and bake at 350°F/180°C for 50-55 minutes or until filling is firm.

Pear and Fig Tart, Deep Dish Chicken Pie

DEEP DISH CHICKEN PIE

Serves 8
Oven temperature 400°F/200°C

- ☐ **2 tablespoons/30 g butter**
- ☐ **4 chicken breast fillets, each weighing approximately 4 oz/125 g**

PASTRY
- ☐ **$2^1/_4$ cups/280 g flour, sifted**
- ☐ **$^1/_2$ cup/125 g butter, chilled**
- ☐ **$^3/_4$ cup/185 g sour cream**

MUSHROOM SAUCE
- ☐ **$^1/_4$ cup/60 g butter**
- ☐ **8 oz/250 g button mushrooms, sliced**
- ☐ **$^1/_4$ cup/30 g flour**
- ☐ **$1^1/_4$ cups/300 mL chicken stock**
- ☐ **3 tablespoons finely chopped fresh parsley**
- ☐ **$^1/_3$ cup/80 mL cream**
- ☐ **2-3 tablespoons white wine**
- ☐ **freshly ground black pepper**
- ☐ **1 egg, lightly beaten**

1 To make pastry, place flour into a large mixing bowl. Rub in butter using fingertips until mixture resembles coarse bread crumbs. Stir in sour cream and mix to form a soft dough. Turn onto a floured surface and knead lightly. Cover and refrigerate for 30 minutes.

2 Melt butter in a skillet and cook chicken for 4-5 minutes each side or until done. Remove from pan and set aside to cool, then cut into cubes.

3 To make sauce, melt butter in a large saucepan and cook mushrooms over a medium heat for 4-5 minutes, or until soft. Remove mushrooms from pan using a slotted spoon and set aside to drain on paper towels.

4 Add flour to pan and cook for 1 minute. Remove pan from heat and gradually blend in stock. Cook over a medium heat, stirring constantly until mixture boils and thickens. Stir in parsley, cream, wine and mushrooms. Season to taste with black pepper. Set aside to cool.

5 Roll out two-thirds of pastry, and line the base and sides of a greased, deep 8 in/ 20 cm pie dish with it.

6 Fill pastry shell with alternate layers of chicken and sauce. Roll out remaining pastry to fit top of pie. Brush edges of pastry shell with water, cover with pastry top. Trim edges, then make slits in top of pie to allow steam to escape. Brush top with egg and bake for 25-35 minutes or until golden.

full of GOODNESS

Soups for all seasons

*F*illing and nutritious soups, broths
and potages have always been the mainstay
of the family diet. The basis of a really
tasty soup is a good stock so it is well worth
making your own. In this chapter you
will find recipes for Hearty Vegetable
Soup, Red Onion Soup and Potato
Bacon Chowder.

Top: Wheat weaving 'Triple Love'
Left: Hearty Vegetable Soup, Creamy Beef
and Mushroom Soup, Red Onion Soup (all
recipes page 64)

taking STOCK

🔊 Stocks based on raw bones have the best flavor and make full-bodied, clear broth that gels on cooling.

🔊 Do not use starchy vegetables, such as potatoes, turnips or parsnips when making stock as they will make it cloudy. Cauliflower, broccoli and cabbage are too strongly flavored to be used in stocks.

🔊 Do not season stock with salt. As stock is an ingredient in other recipes it is better to season the finished dish.

🔊 Using a deep pan will keep evaporation to a minimum.

🔊 Skim off the scum that rises to the surface during cooking.

🔊 Skim fat from surface of stock and strain at the end of cooking. Remove fat by dragging strips of paper towel across the surface, or by chilling the stock until the fat solidifies – it can then be lifted off and discarded.

🔊 Cool stock before covering. To cool rapidly, place pan in a pan of ice cubes and stir.

🔊 You can keep stock in the refrigerator for 3-4 days, or in the freezer for up to 6 months.

BASIC STOCK

To make a basic stock, place 1 lb/500 g marrow bones, cut into pieces, or 1 chicken carcass, skin removed and trimmed of all visible fat; 1 onion, cut into quarters; 2 carrots, chopped; 2 stalks celery, chopped; fresh herbs of your choice; 6 black peppercorns; and 12 cups (3 liters) water in large saucepan or stock pot. Bring to a boil, then reduce heat and simmer for 2 hours, stirring occasionally. Strain stock and refrigerate overnight. Skim fat from surface of stock.

HEARTY VEGETABLE SOUP

Serves 6

- ☐ $^1/_2$ cup/100 g pearl barley
- ☐ 6 cups/1.5 liters water
- ☐ 3 tablespoons/45 g butter
- ☐ 1 large onion, chopped
- ☐ 2 cloves garlic, crushed
- ☐ 1 large carrot, sliced
- ☐ 1 large potato, cubed
- ☐ 3 stalks celery, sliced
- ☐ 1 turnip, diced
- ☐ 1 large parsnip, diced
- ☐ 5 tomatoes, peeled, seeded and chopped
- ☐ $^3/_4$ cup/185 mL tomato puree
- ☐ $^1/_4$ cup finely chopped fresh coriander

1 Place barley and water in a large bowl and set aside to stand overnight.
2 Melt butter in a large heavy-based saucepan and cook onion and garlic over a low heat for 5 minutes or until onion is soft.
3 Add carrot, potato, celery, turnip, parsnip, tomatoes, tomato puree, barley and soaking water to pan. Bring to a boil, then reduce heat and simmer, stirring occasionally, for 20 minutes or until vegetables are tender.
4 Ladle soup into bowls, sprinkle with coriander and serve immediately.

RED ONION SOUP

The secret to this wonderful soup is in the slow cooking of the onions and garlic at the beginning.

Serves 6

- ☐ $^1/_4$ cup/60 g butter
- ☐ 4 teaspoons olive oil
- ☐ 4 large red onions, sliced
- ☐ 12 whole cloves garlic, peeled
- ☐ 3 tablespoons flour
- ☐ 1 teaspoon sugar
- ☐ 2 x 14 oz/440 g canned beef consommé
- ☐ 3 cups/750 mL water
- ☐ $^1/_3$ cup/60 mL red wine
- ☐ 4 teaspoons brandy
- ☐ 1 long bread stick, cut into 12 slices
- ☐ $^1/_4$ cup/60 g melted butter
- ☐ 2 cups/250 g grated sharp cheese
- ☐ 2 tablespoons chopped fresh parsley

1 Heat butter and oil in a large, heavy-based saucepan and cook onions and garlic over a low heat for 15-20 minutes or until onions are golden.
2 Add flour and cook over a medium heat, stirring constantly until flour turns a light straw colour. Stir in sugar, consommé, water, wine and brandy. Bring to a boil, then reduce heat and simmer, stirring occasionally, for 30 minutes.
3 Brush bread slices on both sides with butter. Place under a preheated broiler and toast one side. Sprinkle untoasted side of bread slices with cheese and return to broiler until cheese melts.
4 Place 2 slices of bread into each serving bowl. Ladle soup over bread and sprinkle with parsley. Serve immediately.

CREAMY BEEF AND MUSHROOM SOUP

Serves 6

- ☐ 3 tablespoons vegetable oil
- ☐ $1^1/_2$ lb/750 g lean chuck steak, cut into $^1/_2$ in/1 cm cubes
- ☐ $^1/_4$ cup/60 g butter
- ☐ 4 carrots, sliced
- ☐ 2 leeks, sliced
- ☐ 11 oz/350 g button mushrooms, sliced
- ☐ 2 cloves garlic, crushed
- ☐ 4 tablespoons flour
- ☐ 8 cups/2 liters beef stock
- ☐ 3 tablespoons sherry
- ☐ 4 potatoes, peeled and diced
- ☐ sour cream
- ☐ 2-3 tablespoons snipped fresh chives

1 Heat oil in a large, heavy-based saucepan and cook meat in batches over a medium heat until browned on all sides. Remove meat from pan and set aside.
2 Melt butter in pan and cook carrots and leeks over a low heat for 5 minutes or until leeks are soft. Add mushrooms and garlic and cook for 4-5 minutes longer.
3 Stir in flour and cook for 1 minute. Remove pan from heat and gradually blend in stock and sherry. Bring to a boil, then reduce heat. Return meat to pan with potatoes and simmer for 30 minutes or until meat is tender.
4 Ladle soup into serving bowls, top with a spoonful of sour cream and sprinkle with chives.

VEAL AND HERB DUMPLING SOUP

A hearty soup that is a meal in itself.

Serves 6

- ☐ ¹/₄ cup/60 g butter
- ☐ 2 onions, chopped
- ☐ 4 slices bacon, trimmed of fat and chopped
- ☐ 1¹/₂ lb/750 g lean veal, cut into thin strips
- ☐ ¹/₂ cup/60 g flour, sifted
- ☐ 4 teaspoons paprika
- ☐ 8 cups/2 liters beef stock
- ☐ 2 red peppers, halved and roasted
- ☐ 5 tablespoons tomato paste
- ☐ 4 teaspoons caraway seeds
- ☐ freshly ground black pepper
- ☐ 2-3 tablespoons finely chopped fresh coriander

HERB DUMPLINGS
- ☐ 2 cups/250 g self-rising flour, sifted
- ☐ ¹/₄ cup/60 g butter, cut into small pieces
- ☐ 2 eggs, lightly beaten
- ☐ ¹/₃ cup/80 mL milk
- ☐ 2-3 tablespoons chopped fresh herbs, such as parsley, coriander, rosemary or thyme

1 Melt butter in a large, heavy-based saucepan and cook onions and bacon over a medium-high heat for 4-5 minutes or until bacon is crisp. Using a slotted spoon remove from pan and set aside.

2 Add veal to pan in small batches and cook over a medium heat to brown all sides. Remove from pan and drain on paper towels.

3 Combine flour and paprika. Add to pan and cook over a medium heat for 1 minute. Remove pan from heat and gradually blend in stock. Return onion mixture and meat to pan. Bring to a boil, then reduce heat and simmer for 1¹/₂ hours or until meat is tender.

4 Remove skin from red pepper and chop. Add red pepper, tomato paste and caraway seeds to pan and simmer for 15 minutes longer. Season to taste with black pepper.

5 To make dumplings, place flour in a large mixing bowl. Rub in butter with fingertips until mixture resembles coarse bread crumbs. Combine eggs, milk and herbs. Pour into flour mixture and mix to a smooth dough. Shape tablespoons of mixture into small balls. Cook dumplings in boiling water in a large saucepan for 10-12 minutes or until they rise to the surface. Remove dumplings using a slotted spoon. To serve, place a few dumplings in each bowl, ladle soup over and sprinkle with coriander. Serve immediately.

Cook's tip: To roast peppers, place them under a hot broiler and cook until the skin blisters and chars. Place in a paper or freezer bag and leave for 10 minutes or until cool enough to handle. The skins will then slip off.

Veal and Herb Dumpling Soup

'Miss Dorothy'

CURRIED CHICKEN SOUP

Serves 6

- ☐ ¹/₄ cup/60 g butter
- ☐ 2 onions, chopped
- ☐ 2 cloves garlic, crushed
- ☐ 2 large parsnips, chopped
- ☐ 4 stalks celery, chopped
- ☐ 4 tablespoons flour
- ☐ 4 teaspoons curry powder
- ☐ 6 cups/1.5 liters chicken stock
- ☐ 1¹/₂ cups/185 g fresh or frozen green peas
- ☐ 1 lb/500 g chopped, cooked chicken
- ☐ 8 oz/250 g sour cream
- ☐ ¹/₄ cup finely chopped fresh flat leaf parsley
- ☐ 3 tablespoons chopped fresh dill

1 Melt butter in a large saucepan, cook onions, garlic, parsnips and celery over a low heat for 5-6 minutes or until vegetables are soft. Stir in flour and curry powder and cook for 1 minute longer.

2 Remove pan from heat and gradually blend in stock. Cook over a medium heat, stirring constantly until mixture boils and thickens. Reduce heat, and stir in peas and chicken and cook for 10 minutes.

3 Remove pan from heat and whisk in sour cream, then stir in parsley and dill. Cook over a low heat, stirring frequently, for 3-4 minutes or until warmed through. Serve immediately.

PEA AND SALAMI SOUP

Variations of this soup have been around since the Middle Ages. This one with salami is perfect for a fireside supper.

Serves 6

- ☐ 3 cups/750 g dried split peas, rinsed
- ☐ 16 cups/4 liters water
- ☐ 1 lb/500 g ham bones
- ☐ 4 onions, finely chopped
- ☐ ¹/₃ cup chopped celery leaves
- ☐ 4 stalks celery, chopped
- ☐ ¹/₂ lb/250 g salami, cut into ¹/₂ in/1 cm cubes
- ☐ freshly ground black pepper

1   Place split peas and water in a large, heavy-based saucepan.

2   Add ham bones to pan with peas. Bring to a boil, then reduce heat and simmer for 2 hours or until soup thickens.

3   Stir in onion, celery leaves and celery and cook over a low heat for 20 minutes longer.

4   Remove ham bones from soup and discard. Add salami and cook until heated through. Season to taste with black pepper.

5   Ladle soup into serving bowls.

POTATO BACON CHOWDER

Serves 6

- ☐ $^1/_2$ lb/250 g bacon, chopped
- ☐ 2 tablespoons/30 g butter
- ☐ 2 large onions, chopped
- ☐ 4 stalks celery, chopped
- ☐ 2 teaspoons dried thyme
- ☐ 3 tablespoons flour
- ☐ 6 cups/1.5 liters chicken stock
- ☐ 2 large potatoes, peeled and cubed
- ☐ $1^1/_4$ cups/300 g sour cream
- ☐ $^1/_4$ cup chopped fresh parsley
- ☐ 3 tablespoons snipped fresh chives

1   Place bacon in a large, heavy-based saucepan and cook over a medium heat for 5 minutes or until golden and crisp. Remove from pan and drain on paper towels.

2   Melt butter in pan and cook onions, celery and thyme over a low heat for 4-5 minutes or until onion is soft.

3   Return bacon to pan, then stir in flour and cook for 1 minute. Remove pan from heat and gradually blend in stock. Bring to a boil, then reduce heat. Add potatoes and cook for 10 minutes or until potatoes are tender.

4   Remove pan from heat and stir in sour cream and parsley. Return to heat and cook without boiling, stirring constantly, for 1-2 minutes. Ladle soup into bowls, sprinkle with chives and serve immediately.

Left: Curried Chicken Soup,
Pea and Salami Soup
Right: Potato Bacon Chowder

Tiles Country Floors

family FAVORITES

Desserts and custards

*I*n times past, dessert was served to give energy and bulk. This tradition has fallen from favor as eating habits have changed. However, for a special treat or as a way to satisfy those hungry teenagers, Wild Berry Trifle or Orange and Lemon Delicious Pudding will always remain firm favorites with the family.

Top: Wheat weaving 'Drop Dolly'
Right: Lavender Honey Cream, Butterscotch Cake, Wild Berry Trifle (all recipes page 70)

WILD BERRY TRIFLE

Layers of sponge cake soaked in sherry or fruit juice, fresh berries, strawberry jelly and homemade custard topped with cream make this wonderful trifle.

Serves 8

- [ ] **3 oz/90 g strawberry gelatine crystals**
- [ ] **1 prepared sponge cake**
- [ ] **$^1/_2$ cup/155 g strawberry jam**
- [ ] **$^1/_2$ cup/125 mL sherry or fruit juice**
- [ ] **8 oz/250 g strawberries, hulled and halved**
- [ ] **6$^1/_2$ oz/200 g blueberries**
- [ ] **6$^1/_2$ oz/200 g raspberries**
- [ ] **$^3/_4$ cup/185 mL heavy cream, whipped**

CUSTARD
- [ ] **3 tablespoons vanilla pudding powder blended with $^1/_2$ cup/125 mL milk**
- [ ] **2$^1/_2$ cups/625 mL milk**
- [ ] **$^1/_2$ cup/125 g sugar**
- [ ] **2 eggs, separated**
- [ ] **$^1/_4$ cup/60 mL heavy cream, whipped**

1   Make up gelatine according to package directions. Refrigerate until set.
2   Cut cake into slices, spread with jam, sprinkle with sherry and set aside. Place strawberries, blueberries and raspberries in a bowl and toss to combine. Set aside.
3   To make custard, place vanilla pudding powder mixture, milk and sugar in a saucepan and cook over a low heat, stirring constantly, for 10 minutes or until mixture boils and thickens. Remove pan from heat and whisk in egg yolks. Place a sheet of plastic food wrap directly on the custard to prevent a skin forming. Set aside to cool.
4   Place egg whites in a mixing bowl and beat until stiff peaks form. Stir half the egg whites into the cooled custard. Fold remaining egg whites and cream alternately into custard. Chop jelly roughly into cubes and set aside.
5   To assemble, arrange half the cake slices in the base of a large serving dish, top with half the custard, then half the jelly and half the berries. Repeat layers, finishing with a layer of berries. Decorate top of trifle with cream and refrigerate several hours or overnight before serving.
Cook's tip: Any fresh berries can be used in this dessert. You might like to try blackberries or boysenberries.

LAVENDER HONEY CREAM

Lavender adds a special flavor to this honey cream. Decorate the dessert with fresh lavender flowers.

Serves 6

- [ ] **3 tablespoons dried lavender flowers**
- [ ] **$^1/_4$ cup/60 mL boiling water**
- [ ] **8 egg yolks**
- [ ] **$^1/_4$ cup/60 g superfine sugar**
- [ ] **2 cups/500 mL heavy cream**
- [ ] **$^3/_4$ cup/185 g honey**
- [ ] **2 egg whites**

1   Sprinkle lavender flowers over boiling water and set aside to stand for 30 minutes. Strain and reserve liquid.
2   Place egg yolks and sugar in the top of a double boiler and beat until light and fluffy. Stir in 1 cup/250 mL cream, then place over a saucepan of simmering water and cook, stirring constantly until mixture thickens.
3   Remove top pan from heat and blend in reserved lavender liquid and $^1/_4$ cup honey. Set aside to cool at room temperature.
4   Place remaining cream in a mixing bowl and beat until soft peaks form. Fold through egg yolk mixture. Beat egg whites until stiff peaks form and fold through egg yolk mixture.
5   Spoon into six individual serving dishes and refrigerate until firm. Just prior to serving, drizzle with remaining honey.

BUTTERSCOTCH CAKE

Serves 8

- [ ] **3 eggs**
- [ ] **$^3/_4$ cup/170 g superfine sugar**
- [ ] **$^3/_4$ cup/185 mL milk**
- [ ] **2 teaspoons vanilla extract**
- [ ] **2 cups/250 g self-rising flour**
- [ ] **1 cup/125 g flour**
- [ ] **1 teaspoon baking powder**
- [ ] **$^1/_4$ cup/60 g butter, melted**

BUTTERSCOTCH SAUCE
- [ ] **1 cup/250 g sugar**
- [ ] **$^1/_4$ cup/60 mL water**
- [ ] **$^1/_4$ cup/60 g butter, chopped into small pieces**
- [ ] **2 oz/60 g walnuts, chopped**
- [ ] **1 tablespoon brandy (optional)**

CUSTARD
- [ ] **1 cup/220 g superfine sugar**
- [ ] **1 cup/250 mL water**
- [ ] **4 egg yolks**
- [ ] **$^3/_4$ cup/185 mL heavy cream, whipped**
- [ ] **$^1/_4$ cup/60 mL brandy (optional)**

1   To make sauce, place sugar and water in a saucepan and cook over a low heat, stirring constantly, until sugar dissolves. Bring to a boil and boil without stirring until a light golden color.
2   Remove pan from heat and stir in butter, walnuts and brandy, if using. Cook over a low heat for 2-3 minutes or until butter melts and sauce is smooth. Pour sauce into a greased and wax-paper-lined 8 cup (2 liter) pudding mold.
3   Place eggs and sugar in a large mixing bowl and beat until light and fluffy. Add milk and vanilla extract and beat until combined. Sift together flours and baking powder. Fold flour mixture and melted butter alternately into egg mixture. Spoon into pudding mold, cover with a greased round of wax paper, then seal with lid. Place pudding mold into a large saucepan with enough boiling water to come halfway up the sides of mold. Cook over a medium heat for 1$^1/_4$ hours or until cooked when tested with a skewer. Add more boiling water to pan during cooking, if necessary.
4   To make custard, place sugar and water in a saucepan and cook over a low heat, stirring constantly, until sugar dissolves. Bring to a boil, then reduce heat and simmer, without stirring, for 10 minutes. Place egg yolks in a large mixing bowl and beat until light and fluffy. Pour in sugar syrup in thin stream, beating continuously, until mixture thickens. Fold in cream and brandy, if using.
5   Turn pudding onto a serving plate and serve warm with custard.

CHOCOLATE MALTED SELF-SAUCING PUDDING

This wonderful pudding makes enough for everyone to enjoy second helpings.

Serves 8
Oven temperature 350°F/180°C

- ☐ **1 cup/125 g self-rising flour**
- ☐ **1 cup/125 g flour**
- ☐ **1 teaspoon baking powder**
- ☐ **¹/₄ cup/30 g cocoa powder**
- ☐ **¹/₄ cup/30 g malted milk powder**
- ☐ **1 cup/220 g superfine sugar**
- ☐ **1 cup/250 mL milk**
- ☐ **2 eggs, lightly beaten**

CHOCOLATE SAUCE
- ☐ **3¹/₂ oz/100 g semisweet chocolate, chopped into small pieces**
- ☐ **2 cups/500 mL hot water**
- ☐ **2 tablespoons/30 g butter**
- ☐ **1 cup/170 g brown sugar**
- ☐ **¹/₄ cup/30 g cocoa powder, sifted**
- ☐ **3 tablespoons corn starch**
- ☐ **malted milk powder**
- ☐ **whipped cream**

1 Sift together flours, baking powder, cocoa and malted milk powders into a large mixing bowl. Stir in sugar. Combine milk and eggs and stir into flour mixture. Mix well to combine. Spoon batter into a greased 8 cup (2 litre) capacity ovenproof dish.

2 To make sauce, place chocolate, water and butter in a saucepan and cook over a low heat, stirring constantly until chocolate melts.

3 Place brown sugar, cocoa powder and corn starch in a mixing bowl, pour in chocolate mixture and mix well to combine. Spoon evenly over batter in dish and bake for 45-50 minutes or until firm. Dust top with malted milk powder and serve with whipped cream.

Chocolate Malted Self-Saucing Pudding

'Tsuto'
Rural Japanese packaging

ALMOND CHEESECAKE

Serves 8
Oven temperature 300°F/150°C

- [ ] 3/4 cup/170 g superfine sugar
- [ ] 1/4 cup/60 g butter, softened
- [ ] 16 oz/500 g cream cheese
- [ ] 1/4 cup/30 g flour, sifted
- [ ] 2 tablespoons honey
- [ ] 5 eggs, separated
- [ ] 1/2 cup/125 mL heavy cream
- [ ] 1 teaspoon vanilla extract
- [ ] 1/2 cup/75 g blanched almonds, finely chopped

BROWN SUGAR TOPPING
- [ ] 1/4 cup/45 g brown sugar
- [ ] 1/4 cup/37 g finely chopped blanched almonds
- [ ] 1 teaspoon ground cinnamon

1   To make topping, place brown sugar, almonds and cinnamon in a bowl and mix to combine. Set aside.
2   Place sugar and butter in a bowl and beat until light and fluffy. Add cream cheese and beat until mixture is creamy. Add flour, honey and egg yolks and beat well to combine, then fold in cream and vanilla extract. Place egg whites in a bowl and beat until stiff peaks form. Fold egg whites and almonds into cream cheese mixture.
3   Spoon into a greased and lined 10 in/25 cm springform pan. Sprinkle with topping and cook for 1 1/2 hours or until just firm. Leave cheesecake to cool in turned off oven.
Cook's note: This cheesecake will sink a little on cooling.

APPLE AND RHUBARB CRISP

Serves 4
Oven temperature 350°F/180°C

- [ ] 8 stalks rhubarb, cut into 2 in/5 cm pieces
- [ ] 4 cooking apples, cored, peeled and sliced
- [ ] 1/2 cup/100 g superfine sugar
- [ ] 1/2 cup/125 mL water
- [ ] 1/4 cup/60 mL freshly squeezed orange juice

HAZELNUT CRUMB TOPPING
- [ ] 1/2 cup/100 g ground hazelnuts
- [ ] 1/2 cup/45 g rolled oats
- [ ] 1/4 cup shredded coconut
- [ ] 1/3 cup/45 g flour
- [ ] 1/4 cup/45 g brown sugar
- [ ] 1/4 teaspoon ground cinnamon
- [ ] 6 tablespoons/90 g butter, chopped into small pieces

1   Place rhubarb, apples, superfine sugar, water and orange juice in a saucepan and cook over a medium heat, stirring constantly, until sugar dissolves. Bring to a boil, then reduce heat, cover and simmer for 10 minutes or until fruit is tender. Spoon fruit mixture into a 3 cup/750 mL capacity ovenproof dish.
2   To make topping, combine hazelnuts, oats, coconut, flour, brown sugar and cinnamon in a bowl. Rub in butter using fingertips until mixture resembles coarse bread crumbs. Sprinkle topping over fruit mixture and bake for 20-25 minutes.

COLLEGE PUDDING

College Pudding, the first pudding to be boiled in a cloth, was served to Cambridge University students in 1617.

Serves 4

- [ ] 1/4 cup/75 g strawberry jam
- [ ] 1/4 cup/60 g butter, softened
- [ ] 1/4 cup/60 g superfine sugar
- [ ] 1 egg, lightly beaten
- [ ] 1/2 teaspoon vanilla extract
- [ ] 1 cup/125 g flour
- [ ] 1 teaspoon baking powder
- [ ] 1/3 cup/80 mL milk

1   Place jam in base of a greased and wax-paper-lined 4 cup (1 liter) pudding mold.
2   Place butter and sugar in a mixing bowl and beat until creamy. Add egg and vanilla extract and beat until light and fluffy.
3   Sift together flour and baking powder. Fold flour mixture and milk alternately into egg mixture. Spoon batter into prepared mold.
4   Cover top of pudding with a greased round of wax paper, then seal with lid. Place mold in a large saucepan with enough boiling water to come halfway up the sides of mold. Cook over a medium heat for 1 1/2 hours or until cooked when tested with a skewer. Add more boiling water to pan during cooking, if necessary.

Almond Cheesecake, Apple and Rhubarb Crisp, College Pudding

country FRUIT

An apple tree, a pear tree and a strawberry patch all provide fresh fruits that form the basis of so many country-style recipes. They are also among some of the oldest recorded fruit.

Apples: There are over 7000 varieties of apples in the world today. They were gathered by Stone Age man and cultivated by the ancient Greeks, Romans and Egyptians. Apples team well with many other fruits, especially plums, quinces, rhubarb and apricots. If you have only a small quantity of a more exotic fruit, mix it with apple and you will still retain the exotic flavor.

ta If peeled apples are soaked in cold water with a tablespoon of lemon juice for 15 minutes they will remain pale when cooked.
ta The easiest way to slice apples neatly is to core them first, then peel, halve and finally cut into even slices.

Pears: This fruit has been cultivated since ancient times. As a member of the rose family, a pear, when ripe, understandably has a special scent of its own.

ta Keep pears in a cool place and check them daily, as they ripen very quickly. Overripe pears are tasteless and wooly.
ta Pears are ready to eat when they have a subtle scent and will yield to slight pressure at the stalk.

Strawberries: When purchasing strawberries, choose fresh clean-looking berries with bright green hulls. To clean strawberries, place fruit in a single layer on a damp cloth, roll up and shake gently. Any dirt or dust will be picked up by the cloth. Always clean fruit before hulling.

PEAR AND WALNUT UPSIDE-DOWN CAKE

Serves 8
Oven temperature 350°F/180°C

- ☐ $^1/_4$ cup/60 g raw sugar
- ☐ 2 x 14 oz/440 g canned pear halves, drained and 1 cup/250 mL syrup reserved
- ☐ 8 red glace cherries, halved
- ☐ 1 cup/250 g butter, softened
- ☐ 4 eggs
- ☐ 2 cups/250 g self-rising flour
- ☐ 1 cup/220 g superfine sugar
- ☐ 1 cup/125 g chopped walnuts
- ☐ $^1/_4$ cup/90 g maple syrup

1 Sprinkle base of a greased and lined, deep 9 in/23 cm round cake pan with raw sugar. Arrange pears and cherries over base.

2 Place butter, eggs, flour and sugar in food processor and process until smooth. Stir in walnuts. Carefully spoon batter over pears and cherries in pan and bake for 1-1$^1/_4$ hours, or until cooked when tested with a skewer.

3 Place maple syrup and reserved pear juice in a small saucepan and cook over a medium heat until syrup is reduced by half.

4 Turn cake onto a serving plate and pour over syrup. Serve hot or warm with cream or ice cream if desired.

Sprinkle base of cake pan with raw sugar. Arrange pears and cherries over base.

Carefully spoon batter over pears and cherries in pan.

Bowl and pudding basin Accoutrement

RUM BREAD AND BUTTER PUDDING

This is an exotic version of a family favorite. Allowing the pudding to stand for an hour before baking will give a light crusty texture.

Serves 6
Oven temperature 350°F/180°C

- ☐ ¹/₄ **cup golden raisins**
- ☐ ¹/₄ **cup raisins**
- ☐ **3 tablespoons dark rum**
- ☐ **3 eggs**
- ☐ **3 egg yolks**
- ☐ ³/₄ **cup/170 g superfine sugar**
- ☐ **3 cups/750 mL milk**
- ☐ **1 cup/250 mL cream**
- ☐ **2 teaspoons vanilla extract**
- ☐ **4 teaspoons finely grated orange rind**
- ☐ **12 slices buttered bread, crusts removed and slices cut into quarters**
- ☐ **1 teaspoon ground cinnamon**

1   Place raisins in a bowl, pour over rum and set aside to soak for 30 minutes.

2   Combine eggs, egg yolks and ¹/₂ cup/ 100 g sugar in a mixing bowl and beat until light and fluffy. Place milk and cream in a saucepan and cook over a medium heat, stirring constantly, until almost boiling. Remove pan from heat and set aside to cool slightly. Pour milk mixture into egg mixture and beat until combined. Blend in vanilla extract and orange rind.

3   Place one-third of the bread slices, buttered side up, in a greased 8 cup (2 liter) capacity ovenproof dish. Top with half raisin mixture. Repeat with remaining bread and raisin mixture, finishing with a layer of bread, buttered side facing up.

4   Pour egg mixture evenly over bread in dish. Combine remaining sugar with cinnamon and sprinkle over pudding. Bake for 1 hour or until a knife inserted in the center comes out clean.

Cook's note: The rum may be omitted from this pudding.

Rum Bread and Butter Pudding

ORANGE AND LEMON DELICIOUS PUDDING

One of those magic puddings – as the pudding cooks it separates to give a layer of fluffy sponge over a tangy citrus sauce.

Serves 6
Oven temperature 350°F/180°C

- ☐ **1 cup/220 g superfine sugar**
- ☐ **¹/₂ cup/125 g butter, softened**
- ☐ **¹/₂ cup/60 g self-rising flour**
- ☐ **4 teaspoons finely grated lemon rind**
- ☐ **4 teaspoons finely grated orange rind**
- ☐ **2 tablespoons lemon juice**
- ☐ **3 tablespoons freshly squeezed orange juice**
- ☐ **2 eggs, separated**
- ☐ **1 cup/250 mL milk**

1 Place sugar and butter in a bowl and beat until light and fluffy. Mix in flour, lemon rind, orange rind, lemon juice and orange juice.

2 Place egg yolks and milk in a small bowl and whisk to combine. Mix into citrus mixture.

3 Beat egg whites until stiff peaks form then fold into batter. Spoon into a greased 4 cup/1 litre capacity ovenproof dish. Place dish in a baking pan with enough boiling water to come halfway up the side of dish. Bake for 45 minutes or until cooked. Serve hot with cream or ice cream.

Orange and Lemon Delicious Pudding

INDEX

WHEAT WEAVINGS
The publisher would like to thank Nonie McFarlane for the Wheat Weavings used throughout this book. Nonie is a specialist in Straw Craft and is a member of The Society of Arts and Crafts of New South Wales and the British Guild of Straw Craftsmen. Nonie has attended The Straw Craft Centre, Much Cowarne, Herefordshire, England and her work is now considered to be in the Master Class category.

Handy reminders . . .

PREPARING THE CAKE PANS

To grease and flour a cake pan: Using a pastry brush lightly brush cake pan with melted butter or margarine, then sprinkle with flour and shake to coat evenly. Invert pan on work surface and tap gently to remove excess flour.

To grease and line a round cake pan: Place cake pan on a large piece of parchment or wax paper; using a pencil trace around the base, then cut out shape. Grease pan and line with paper.

To line a deep cake pan: A deep cake pan should be lined on the bottom and sides. Use a double-thickness folded strip of wax paper 2 in/5 cm higher than the cake pan and long enough to fit around the pan and to overlap by about 1 in/2.5 cm. On the folded edge turn up about 1 in/2.5 cm and crease, then using scissors snip at regular intervals across the flap as far as the fold. Cut out a piece of wax paper to line the bottom of the pan as described above. Grease the pan and place the strip inside it with the snipped flap lying flat on the bottom. Be sure that the ends overlap so that the sides are completely covered by the paper. Place the other piece of wax paper in the pan to cover the snipped flap.

To line a loaf pan: Cut a strip of wax paper the width of the base of the pan and long enough to come up the shorter sides of the pan and extend by 1 in/2.5 cm. Grease the pan and line with the paper. When the cake is done the unlined sides can be loosened with a knife and the paper ends used to lift out the cake.

US/CANADIAN SUGAR SUBSTITUTES

If the recipe calls for:	You can use:
Superfine sugar	Caster sugar, or place granulated sugar in a food processor or blender and process to make finer.
Raw sugar	Demerara or muscovado sugar
Confectioners' sugar	Icing sugar

US/CANADIAN FLOUR SUBSTITUTES

If the recipe calls for:	You can use:
Self-rising flour	All-purpose flour: For every cup of flour add one teaspoon baking powder
Cake flour	All-purpose flour or a mixture of flour and cornstarch. For 1 cup/125 g flour, replace 2 tablespoons with cornstarch, sift the flours together to ensure that they are well mixed

HANDY REMINDERS

3 teaspoons = 1 tablespoon = 15 mL
($1/3$ tablespoon = 1 teaspoon)
4 tablespoons = $1/4$ cup = 60 mL

When measuring butter:

1 tablespoon = 15 g = $1/2$ oz
4 tablespoons = 60 g = 2 oz = $1/4$ cup = $1/2$ stick
8 tablespoons = 125 g = 4 oz = $1/2$ cup = 1 stick

All amounts specified in ounces (oz) indicate weight; these are not fluid ounces and may or may not be equivalent to measuring cup/spoon volume.

Flour is assumed to be all-purpose unless otherwise indicated.

Chocolate is assumed to be sweetened.

Cocoa powder is assumed to be unsweetened.

T3-BAG-921

7   24976 00795   4

ISBN 1-56197-037

U.S. $7.95/CANADA $9.95